The Story of Isabel Bevier

the story of

Isabel Bevier

Lita Bane

PUBLICATIONS

Chas. A. Bennett Co., Inc., Peoria, Illinois

921
B∦68b
c.1

I believe that all of us become better citizens, richer and better directed human beings, through a knowledge of the dreams and deeds of the men and women who went before.

A. B. GUTHRIE, JR.

Preface

THERE ARE persons whose traits of mind and heart would enable them to live helpfully in any age. Isabel Bevier was such a person. Her eagerness to use her every talent to make life, especially home life, rich and rewarding would in itself have given her distinction. Her success in helping to launch a large and important movement devoted to this high purpose has given her a certain universality and timelessness.

The University of Illinois chapter of Phi Upsilon Omicron believed that some record should be made of her life. That is how this book came to be. Its contents were chosen in an effort to point out the way she trod and to make as real as possible the woman who chose that way.

The best way to accomplish this purpose posed a difficult problem, so elusive are the elements needed in a book of this nature. Through the efforts of the active chapter, its faculty advisers, and alumnae, funds were raised, material collected, and attempts made at different times by professional friends of Isabel Bevier to write a book about her. Each time all were agreed that the story fell short of its mark and would not accomplish what the sponsoring group had hoped for. At last it was decided that the best way to make known what kind of person she was, and what she stood for, was to let her speak for herself for the most part.

At the request of the biography committee, the task of preparing the material for publication fell to my lot. With the help of many interested persons I have carried out my assignment. Selections have been made from Isabel Bevier's published and unpublished writings, and certain statements made by her friends have been used. All collected materials have been preserved for future use.

This book is largely devoted to her twenty-one years as head of the Home Economics Department and vice-director of Home Economics Extension at the University of Illinois. Through the years her ideas, ideals, and standards will be sifted, and those that stand the test of time will be used again and again, not only in directing and strengthening the home economics movement, but in shaping the education of women to fit their changing personal and social responsibilities.

Yet, at best, a book such as this, compiled from many sources, unfortunately leaves some attributes unrecorded. It can be only a partial picture.

Isabel Bevier's most active home economics professional life (1900-1921) paralleled the first years of the organized home economics movement, and she was a person of power and influence in shaping its development. Her life and writings point up the foundations of modern homemaking philosophy and indicate how one of the pioneers developed her ideas and translated them into action.

This interest in homemaking as an area for scientific study resulted not only in the rise of what is known as the home economics movement but added momentum to a general movement toward making scientific facts more generally available and putting them to work for human betterment. Other people in addition to Justice Holmes were seeing the need (as he expressed it) to "make facts live — leap into an organic order, live, and bear fruit."

A book devoted to the life and work of any one individual is bound to raise questions in the mind of the potential reader. Who was this person? Why is she noteworthy? What manner of person was she? What was the nature of the work that won her devotion and in which she served with enough distinction to merit biographical attention?

In these pages you will meet Isabel Bevier — the woman, the scholar, the administrator — as she saw herself and as friends and coworkers saw her. In the second part of the book she speaks mostly for herself, through excerpts from her talks and published articles. By these means we hope to give the reader an insight into the life and work of a woman who possessed the attributes of true greatness.

Believing as she did that "there is an art in a well-ordered home and a well-ordered life," Isabel Bevier left a legacy of rich promise in the broad field of educating men and women for their homemaking responsibilities.

Contents

Chapter I

Days of Preparation

Unfortunately, we have little detailed information about the formative influences in Isabel Bevier's childhood and early youth. The daguerreotype of Isabel at three shows her a serious-eyed little girl with a high forehead and a look of alertness and intelligence. She retained that look all her life. Beyond the picture and her own casual reference to having been born on a farm we know almost nothing about her childhood. (See Eugene Davenport's notes, page 13 and following.)

There must have been some compelling reason for her leaving her farm home to go to preparatory school and college, but our sources leave that information vague. We know from her own account that a profound change in her life came when, after the stunning shock of her fiance's drowning in 1888, she made her decision with the help of friends to enter the field of science.

Although we lack details about Isabel's early years, we can find many motivating influences in what was happening all around her. She was born in 1860 into an atmosphere of thought increasingly favorable to the education of women. Vassar was founded when she was five, and her future teacher and friend, Ellen Swallow Richards, was one of the first students; Smith followed in 1873 and Wellesley in 1875. Her own state of Ohio had led in the movement, Oberlin having been opened as a co-educational college in 1833, almost thirty years before her birth. Wooster, the Presbyterian college from which she graduated, was founded in 1866 when she was starting off to grade school.

Living as she was in a farm home she must have heard talk about the land-grant colleges with their plans for offering practical education to women as well as men. She was two when the first Morrill Act was passed in 1862 and ten when Michigan, California, Missouri, and, significantly, Illinois, took advantage of the grant plan and opened universities for men and women.

A sensitive and perceptive person, Isabel could not escape the impulse which women's education was receiving. She did escape its traditional pattern. At our point in time it is hard to realize what it meant in the 1880's for a woman to venture into the field of science. Languages, art appreciation, music, and literature were considered proper for a woman if she must be educated. There seemed to be almost no thought of applying scientific principles to the work in which most women were engaged — homemaking.

Through her study of science and her friendships with scientists, Isabel was able to see the possibilities of making this application — of using the findings of science to help solve the problems women were meeting every day in their homes. Nutrition was one of them. While at that time little was known about human nutrition, she had been observing and felt sure it had an importance to human well-being not yet appreciated. She concluded too that if women knew something about architecture their homes might be better engineered to fit the needs of family living. With her purpose constantly before her, she studied a fragment here, another there, and put them together to form "household science," as she termed it.

Isabel's Personal Background

As a friend, and as an administrator fully aware of the value of Isabel Bevier's contribution to education, Dean Eugene Davenport of Illinois tells something of the background of her life and career. Speaking first of the significance of her birthplace, a farm near Plymouth, Ohio, he wrote:

"The fact that she began life and spent her early girlhood in a rich and prosperous region at the southwest corner of the Western Reserve helps to account for her subsequent career. Not only was the country rich and prosperous, as riches and prosperity went in those days, but the people were of that sturdy stock that cast their fortunes with the Connecticut Fire Lands and developed there what was probably the most characteristically American of all the civilization centers west of the Alleghenies. The spirit of personal initiative was the distinguishing mark of these sons of pioneers. Of the home-building type, they nevertheless had an early baptism of fire in the War of 1812 and another in the '60's. War to them was not an occupation but a disagreeable necessity in defense of free institutions.

"All this must have had its influence upon the development of a character naturally strong. For in such an environment this farm girl lived all her early life and until she went away to college. She taught country school, which brought her into intimate contact with life as it is actually lived under a variety of conditions. Besides, the Civil War had hit Ohio hard, and the days of recovery were times of intense purposes and of extremely hard work. Both men and women learned what hard work really was.

"And so it was that Isabel Bevier was brought up in a period when nothing seemed too hard if only it was well worth while.

"It seemed written in the book of fate that this farm girl should be very largely dependent upon the friendship and counsel of men. Her choice of science threw her almost entirely with men, for at that time few women were in college and fewer still were studying science. Those were pioneer days in home economics, as they had been shortly before in agriculture."

Dean Davenport speaks of the "sturdy stock" from which Isabel came. The name Bevier is of French origin, her father being of French ancestry, with possibly some Dutch. Her mother was Dutch, a Brinkerhoff. On both sides her ancestors were adventuring, pioneering people.

In 1675 Louis Bevier with his wife and baby came to New Amsterdam. They came from the lower Palatinate, where his people had settled when religious persecution drove the Huguenots from France. After two years at New Amsterdam, Louis and his family joined eleven other Palatinate families in the settling of New Paltz, not far from what is now Poughkeepsie. They prospered.

Today, in New Paltz, New York, in a small, grassy triangle on the original Huguenot Street, a large boulder is inscribed, "To the memory and in honor of the twelve original settlers." The name of Louis Bevier is among those engraved. On this same street, the old Bevier house of stone with a massive Dutch door is still standing, although it passed out of the family's possession in 1735. The historical marker attached to the house indicates the years of Bevier ownership.

Andreas Bevier, direct descendent of Louis, left the homestead and moved west. He settled near Plymouth, Ohio. His son, Caleb, was Isabel Bevier's father.

Isabel herself credited her love of wandering and her spirit of adventure to the Brinkerhoffs, her mother's people. In 1639 Joris Dircksen Brinkerhoff came with his wife from Holland to New Amsterdam. In 1646 he settled in Brooklyn, where he was prominent in affairs of the town and a ruling elder in the church. One of his descendents, Henry Roeliff Brinkerhoff, became General Brinkerhoff and a member of the state legislature. In 1828 he moved his family from New York State to Ohio, settling near Plymouth. His daughter, Cornelia, was Isabel Bevier's mother.

Louis Betts who painted Isabel's portrait, called her a French type. Yet one is inclined to associate her sturdiness with her Dutch progenitors. Whether we think of her as a Bevier or a Brinkerhoff, there is ample evidence that her vitality, her keen mind, and her striking appearance were the fruits of a splendid inheritance.

When preparing his short sketch of Isabel Bevier as part of the material for this book, Dean Davenport asked her for some biographical data. She responded with some pages of what she termed "material facts." This account given in the forthright and unadorned fashion so characteristic of her, is reproduced here virtually in its entirety. She wrote:

Isabel's Autobiographical Notes

"I was born on a farm five miles from anywhere, the

youngest of nine children, in cold weather, in the midst of a rich and populous region, three miles from three churches and five miles from two towns, and really lived there all my life until I went to college. I taught a country school the summer before I was sixteen years of age, and taught for three successive summers before I went to Wooster Preparatory. I had been in the Plymouth [Ohio] High School for two years, but it was not accredited, so I had to go to Wooster Preparatory for two years. My mother died the first year I was in Preparatory, so I could not complete the year. As it seemed better to just go on another year, I was slightly irregular.

"It seems to me most of the changes in my life have come because I did something that somebody else thought I should do. For example, in college I took German and Latin and some French, and was supposed to do my best work in languages. My father's influence got me a position in the Shelby [Ohio] High School, where I was principal for two years; then I went to Mt. Vernon High School and taught mathematics and Latin."

Her record shows her teaching in high school from 1885 through 1888, having graduated from the University of Wooster in 1885 and earned her master's degree at the same institution in 1888. It was in the latter year that tragedy struck, changing her whole life. Her fiance, Elmer Strain, whom she had known at Wooster University, had just completed his course at the Harvard Medical School and was taking a short vacation. While swimming with several companions, he was drowned. She rarely spoke of this tragic experience but when she did, you realized how vivid the memory of it was and something of the depth of her grief. The young men who were with Elmer Strain at the time of

his death and who were also friends of Isabel, corresponded with her through all the succeeding years.

Her account continues:

"Meanwhile, my roommate had married and was living in Pittsburgh, and she and her husband conceived the idea that it would be nice to have me teach in the Pennsylvania College for Women. The vacancy happened to be in the sciences, about which I felt I knew very little, but I decided to try it and so asked if I could study chemistry in Case School of Applied Sciences in Cleveland.

"The request was granted, though there was no summer school; and after I had arrived on the spot and had some acquaintance with my instructor, I was told that I was the only woman who had ever asked to study in Case. I simply knew that it was a good scientific school and wrote for information, and the reply was that Professor Albert W. Smith would be working in oils and could tutor me. It was really a great chance. He had only one other student, who fell by the way, so I went as far and as fast as I could and really learned considerable chemistry. The next year I returned and did likewise.

"During this time I had in Pennsylvania College the large and indefinite title of Professor of Natural Sciences. I taught, in the nine years I was there — chemistry always, geology two years, physics two, botany nine. I had taught that in Mt. Vernon. At the end of two years Professor Smith, whom I consider a good deal of a prophet, told me that the place for women in chemistry was in work with foods, and that the big universities in the Middle West, like Michigan, Wisconsin, and Illinois, would one day have some kind of a department for foods work with women in it, and I should get ready. I should not come to him any more, but I should

17

go to Harvard summer school and then to Professor Atwater's laboratory.

"So, armed with a letter of recommendation from Dr. Mayberry, head of chemistry in Case, I went to Harvard, and the registrar told me that since Dr. Mayberry was a personal friend of his he would do what they usually did not do — he would find me a nice place to live in a fine old New England family. That really meant very much to me because later in the summer Professor Putnam of Peabody Museum at Harvard and his wife came there to visit the family, and Professor Putnam asked me if I was going to work as a chemist in the World's Fair. That Fair was two years away and I had never even dreamed of such a thing.

"Meantime my father died in January, 1893. I had arranged to go to the Fair for ten days with some Pittsburgh friends. The first night when I got home from the Fair there was a telegram asking me to report at the Administration Building. I was much amazed and wondered what had happened since I had forgotten about Professor Putnam. In the morning I found that Mrs. Virginia C. Meredith was one of the powers that be. I had never seen her. She told me that I had been recommended by Professor Putnam as a scientific young woman, and because of his recommendation they had sent for me and would give me a position. I should go on with my plans but call occasionally at the office until the committee could be formed.

"I remember very distinctly how I rushed over to the Museum to Professor Putnam's office and said to him I was very grateful for his recommendation, but I was sure I could not do what they wanted me to. He looked at me rather curiously and said, 'Just what is it they want you to do?' I said, 'I do not really know; they do not know yet." He said,

'Very well, when they really do know, if you can't do it I want you to go home, because I have recommended only three women, and I expect them to do themselves and me credit, but I do not want you to go away until you find out exactly what you are to do.'

"So I went back and followed directions, and the tenth day when my friends were about to depart I was told to get in the elevator and go upstairs; the committee was to be formed. It ended, to the great amusement of the people who knew me, by my being made secretary of the Mineral Waters Committee, and A. A. Breneman of New York City was to be chairman. The plan was to have the power in the hands of Americans, but other people were to be put on; so we had one German, one Mexican, one sugar man from Trinidad, Spain, one doctor, director of an insane asylum in Nebraska, Professor Breneman, and myself. Professor Breneman had to go back to New York to close up his work and to make arrangements to send some of the World's Fair materials to his laboratory and some of them — the greater part of them — went to the chemical department of Northwestern under Long, who was then in charge.

"That was a very interesting experience. I stayed until Pennsylvania College opened, and then, in October, Professor Breneman wrote and asked that I be released for two weeks to finish up the records. That was really the beginning of my acquaintance with Dr. Wiley, Dr. Langworthy, and Professor Atwater. I did work for a few days in the U. S. Chemical Laboratory, weighing samples under Dr. Wiley, but my real work in connection with the World's Fair was done with the Mineral Waters Committee. Needless to say, I greatly enjoyed my experiences with that group. Before that my acquaintance with mineral waters had been confined to an occasional soda.

"I always went to see Professor Smith in the summer, and when I told him about my World's Fair experience, he said, 'Well, now you must go to Professor Atwater's laboratory,' and I said, 'Why, what would he want with me?' Professor Smith said, 'Well, whatever is worth having is worth asking for. You must write and ask him if you can work in his laboratory.' I did write two letters, one to the University of Chicago and one to Professor Atwater. The catalog of the summer work came from Chicago University, and a letter from Professor Atwater which said, 'We have no summer school as such, but my assistants will be here and we shall be glad to have you come and you can have abundant opportunity to work with food with us.'

"So I went for six weeks' work with Dr. Woods, afterward of Maine, head of Professor Atwater's laboratory, and Dr. Langworthy was detailed to look after me. Professor Atwater talked with me, told me of his hopes and fears. He was then director of the agricultural experiment station at Storrs and was trying to get money for his investigations. He asked me what I was interested in and what I would like to work at, and I said, 'bread.' He said he would be very glad to have me get some samples ready and bring them back at the holiday vacation, so I interviewed the head of the U. S. Baking Company, a member of the church I attended, whom I knew slightly.

"I collected samples, dried them, and prepared them. Professor Atwater came to Pittsburgh and we had a dinner for him at the college with the interested people, and then we went to the poorer districts. He was having dietary studies made then in various parts of the United States, and he wanted some made in Pittsburgh, so I made seven there for him, representative of three levels of living. We had the poorest family in Cherry Valley, the most prosperous one in Polish Row, and the family of a very well known Pittsburgh attorney, and two or three between. I spent my holiday vacation in Middletown analyzing my samples of bread and getting my data for the dietary studies in shape.

"By the end of 1897 I had decided that I was not going to teach in a woman's college any longer. The life seemed to be abnormal, so I severed my connection with the college and decided to take a year of study. I arranged to study with Dr. Morley in Western Reserve and took my organic chemistry under that wonderful man. Then I felt better ready for my food work and decided at the middle of the year that I would go to Tech [Massachusetts Institute of Technology] and work with Mrs. Richards, to whom Professor Putnam had introduced me in the summer I was at Harvard.

"I ought to say before I close this chapter that when I was ready to leave that first summer I asked Professor Atwater about my expenses for tuition, chemicals, etc., and he said, 'Nothing!' He said that when he had come back from Europe, keen to do something in the analysis of foods, the man who was then at the head of the United States Fisheries Department had given him his chance to work and he was passing that chance on to me. Also, Mrs. Richards had written me that I could have my tuition in Tech free and work with her in air, water, and food. I took sanitary chemistry with her, sanitary biology and sanitary science with Dr. Sedgwick, and Mrs. Richards had me do special work with a sugar man. So I really had a very good chance in Tech.

"In May Professor Atwater wrote and asked me to go to

21

Hampton to make dietary studies among the Negroes. I was quite appalled at the job and wrote him so, but when I spoke to Mrs. Richards she said, 'Why, of course you will go. You cannot afford professionally not to. Professor Atwater has asked you and it is a great chance.' I heard nothing more from Professor Atwater until a telegram came, asking me to meet him at Young's Hotel to make arrangements to go to Hampton.

"So I say I went to Pennsylvania College because my roommate wanted me to; I went to Harvard and to Professor Atwater because Professor Smith told me to; and I went to Hampton because Mrs. Richards and Professor Atwater told me to.

"Then the summer passed and I had not been recommended for any job that I wanted. The agencies got me jobs to teach zoology. While I had taught that in elementary classes among the numerous ones I taught in Pennsylvania College, I knew I did not know how to teach it, so I decided to go back to Mrs. Richards and work and read, for I had not had time to do the reading I wanted. This account will perhaps help to explain why I have inscribed under the photographs of Dr. Smith, Professor Putnam, Professor Atwater, Dr. True, and Mrs. Richards, 'My bountiful benefactors.'

"Professor Canfield of Ohio State had written asking me if I would start a department of household science or something of the kind at Ohio State. I wrote him that if he was willing to begin in a small way until we could find out what we really could do and wanted to do, I would be glad to do it; but if he wanted a large and spectacular work in the beginning, I should not undertake it. He wrote back that by my own confession I was not prepared. Then I had a good blowing up from Professor Smith, and he said that the next time he got me a job he wanted me to take it. So I decided to go back to Mrs. Richards and her laboratory.

"While I was there and she was on a western trip, I developed a course which I named 'chemistry, with applications to food and physiology,' and took it over to Professor Sedgwick and asked him if he would tell me what he thought of it. I said I was ashamed of the name because it was such a long one, but that was what I meant. He said he would not worry about the length of it if that was what I expected to do.

"When Mrs. Richards came back, I showed her my course and she said, 'Why, you seem to be all ready, and Lake Erie College at Painesville wants a professor of chemistry with such applications as you have.' So I went to Lake Erie College. I confess it was a terrible disappointment to go into a woman's college again, but I went there in November as professor of chemistry. I really never had such a good chance to work for myself because there were few students in general chemistry and I had time to work on my applications and develop my ideas.

"The next year they wished me to plan the menus for the college, give a new course in chemistry and the general one — that is, all the work in chemistry — and have charge of the course in sanitation. Miss Elizabeth Sprague was secured to come as my assistant. So we planned the meals for the hundred and fifteen, and oversaw the domestic arrangements — they had a modified Mt. Holyoke plan with one Negro cook, one English woman to bake, two women to wash the tins, and the girls to do the rest. It was a marvelous experience.

"A plague of typhoid fever in some way came upon us. I spent the month of November at home having what the doctor called malaria fever, the only real sickness I ever had in my life. They extended the Christmas vacation through December, and in January we went back and began again. Meanwhile the manager had proved inefficient, and Miss Sprague and I thought we would run it ourselves. We went through January and made our famous dietary study by weighing every morsel of food and waste for that family of a hundred and fifteen for ten days. Then in February Miss Sprague fell ill. We had to plan the menus a month in advance because the meat which the college used came from Cleveland and was kept in storage in Painesville.

"Finally, the last of February I took Miss Sprague to Cleveland and put her on the train for her home in Cincinnati. Only I was left of that noble force of three to teach chemistry, sanitation, and run the domestic arrangements.

"In the Easter vacation there came word from President Draper that I was to come to Illinois for an interview. Miss Sprague and I had already agreed that we would not stay another year at Painesville and had handed in our resignations. I came, I saw you and President Draper, and was conquered and decided to try out my ideas in the University of Illinois.

"Will you pardon this long chapter and return it to me when you have finished, because I shall never want to tell it over again."

The conference with President Draper resulted in Isabel Bevier's allying her interests with, to quote Dean Davenport, "those of the most rapidly developing university of the western continent."

"With this engagement," continues Davenport, "the period of preparation may be considered as closed and the real life work begun. . . . What was it," he asks, "that led or drove this farm girl along her zigzag course of preparation? Preparation for what? Nobody could have answered the question then, much less she herself. She belongs to a worthy company of pioneers. She worked with pioneers of science, not content to follow beaten trails along the margins of a goodly prospect, but intent upon exploration for themselves. So she caught the spirit of the trail maker, and it led her all the way, 'a pillar of cloud by day and a pillar of fire by night.'"

How well Isabel Bevier's ideas were succeeding by the time she had been a faculty member for six years is indicated in a letter written by President Draper of Illinois to Dean Liberty Hyde Bailey of Cornell University in response to his inquiry about her. President Draper wrote:

President A. S. Draper's Statement

"I know Miss Isabel Bevier and her work very thoroughly, for I first found her trying to develop a department of household science, or home economics, at Lake Erie College, Painesville, Ohio, and brought her to the University of Illinois for the first serious effort to establish such work on a university grade that has really been made in the country.

"At the time of her appointment at Illinois I felt far from certain about her strength, though not about her character or culture and accomplishments, and I was somewhat skeptical as to whether such a department could be established in a university so as to make it really worth the time and cost. With very many obstacles in her way, Miss Bevier steadily pushed her work to success and in time accomplished precisely what I desired.

"What I wished was a university department which would command the respect of other university departments and at the same time make an impression upon the home life of the people, particularly in the farming districts. I wanted a department which was really scientific and knew what it was talking about and could attract students to the fundamental principles upon which the comfort and health-fulness and attractiveness of the home must rest. I cared little about fanciful or spectacular demonstrations in cooking or dressmaking, but a great deal about women being educated so that they would have sound judgment and considerable resourcefulness in determining what a good home needs and how to get it.

"I told Miss Bevier at the beginning that I should not expect her to travel a great deal for the purpose of entertaining people, but that I should expect her to command the interest of students upon such subjects as domestic architecture, and particularly the interior architectural construction of the house, its sanitation, its utility and its attractiveness; the chemistry of foods and their adaptation to the different needs of the members of the family; the uses of clothing, its material, its manufacture and its suitability to the differing conditions in life; as well as all the other things which enter into good homemaking, the competent management of the household and the health and happiness of all in the house.

"I told her that I should not care to have her engage in any work which was not based upon a sound scientific principle; that while it would be desirable for her to elucidate these things now and then before a public audience, it was to be distinctly understood that her main work would be in her laboratories and lecture room, and would be judged by the measure of University respect which she was able to gain for it.

"I have been a little particular in indicating what I had in mind concerning the development of a department of household economics.

"Miss Bevier succeeded beyond my expectations in accomplishing the things which I wanted. If your ideals are substantially the same, she can do it at Cornell more surely than any other woman in the country. . . .

"The department of household economics, as you doubtless know, has just been splendidly housed in the new Woman's Building at the University of Illinois, and everything promises a still larger measure of accomplishment. There are reasons enough why Miss Bevier should remain here; many a university has tried to get her away and been unsuccessful. . . .

"It occurs to me that I have not stated the essential traits of Miss Bevier's personal and professional character. She is a woman of sound and sane religious life, she has marked dignity of bearing, is attractive in person, has passed through very deep sorrows, but is gifted with a sunny temperament which always stands her well in hand. She is thoroughly quick-witted and has a sense of humor which gives her ready welcome to every social circle.

"She is scientifically educated, with chemistry as her major work. She has the scientific habit and method which lead her to go into things with an analytical mind and to rest plans upon a foundation which will stand. She writes very well and appears to good advantage at public gatherings. She is singularly successful in avoiding embarrassing situations in a work which has to deal with people who are both inquisitive and sensitive and which is fraught with many pitfalls.

"She has had very considerable experience since her

graduation from college, as she has worked with Professor Atwater and the United States Department of Agriculture, with several years of teaching at Lake Erie College, and the charge of the first university department of household economics which had developed to anything like a university success.

"With considerable familiarity with the whole subject, I am bound to say that if there is any other woman in the country who approaches Miss Bevier as a builder and leader of such work I have never heard of her."

Such was her president's estimate of Isabel Bevier in 1906.

Chapter II

At the University of Illinois

In 1934 at the request of Director P. L. Windsor of the University of Illinois library, Isabel Bevier prepared a detailed history of her twenty-one years as department head and six years as vice-director of home economics extension, to be filed in the archives. The greater part of this chapter is drawn from this narrative.

First Impressions of a New "Home"

"I shall never forget my first impressions of Champaign that April day when I arrived to be looked over. I was the guest of President Draper, and after luncheon he took me for a drive. I thought I had never seen so flat and so muddy a place: no trees, no hills, no boundaries of any kind. This lack of boundaries, physical and mental, the open-mindedness of the authorities and their willingness to try experiments, indeed their desire to do so, opened up a whole new world to me. President Draper and I soon found one common bond, possibly a surprising one, our love of fine horses. I felt almost as if I had been riding with my father. We went to see Dean Davenport in the house out by the

29

barns, and he and I looked at the new Agricultural Building [Davenport Hall] and talked about farm life and education for it. I remember I told Dean Davenport I had been reared on a 200-acre farm and felt that I knew much of the life that went on there, but Illinois University seemed to be working on the 800-acre basis.

"Then I had a conference with that gentleman of the old school, Dr. Burrill, on education and life, both of which he understood so well. By the time these conferences were completed, I was ready to agree to President Draper's statement, 'We don't have much scenery around here, but we do have a good crowd to live with.'

"There is another vivid memory of that visit. On Sunday afternoon we went to the chapel in University Hall to attend services held in honor of Professor Morrow, Dean Davenport's predecessor. I recall that Professor Stephen A. Forbes made the principal address and that I thought it good (as I learned afterward his addresses were sure to be). But my most vivid memory is of the ugliness of the room, its awkward shape and size, and its color, an awful blue. I could not help contrasting it with the beautiful, new, well-proportioned and well-furnished chapel in Lake Erie College, from which I had come.

"I cherish yet that fateful telegram dated April 19, 1900, which reads:

"'TRUSTEES YESTERDAY ELECTED YOU PROFESSOR OF HOUSEHOLD SCIENCE AT FIFTEEN HUNDRED DOLLARS PER YEAR AND MISS SPRAGUE AT EIGHT HUNDRED. WILL YOU BOTH ACCEPT? A. S. DRAPER.'

"I had long before decided that I would not spend my years teaching in any woman's college, although I had learned much while living in them. But I had never been able to make them seem other than abnormal places of residence for me. My association with my father and three brothers, as well as my training in coeducational colleges, had made me entirely coeducational in all my sympathies. Moreover, these years had given me some rather definite ideas as to what I thought constituted a liberal education for women, and I was pleased to find that I was to have my chance to plan a course that would help me realize my ideals."

The University of Illinois, in which Isabel decided to try out her ideas, had for some years given attention to the education of women. As early as 1869-70 the catalog announced a "Ladies' Department," going on to say: "The trustees have voted to admit female students as soon as suitable accommodations can be provided. Ladies already attend the lecture courses and early preparations will be made to afford them the full benefits of the Institution." The catalog for 1873-74 included a "School of Domestic Science and Arts," and Dr. J. M. Gregory, Regent (President) of the University, recommended to the Board of Trustees "the employment of a lady instructor of the highest attainments and large experience. . . . If a lady can be found who can properly open and direct the studies in the School of Domestic Economy her employment will be of double use and value. . . . In this connection I wish to repeat the recommendation that at the earliest day practicable you provide fully for a School of Domestic Economy and such other schools as the wants of our female students demand."

The "lady of high character and culture" specified by Regent Gregory was found in the person of Miss Lou C.

Allen in 1874. She reports that "the school was the outgrowth of a conviction that a rational system for the higher and better education of women must recognize their distinctive duties as women . . . the mothers, housekeepers, and health keepers of the world . . . and furnish instruction which shall fit them to meet these duties . . . enabling them to bring the aids of science and culture to the all-important labors and vocations of womanhood. . . . If ignorance is a weakness and a disaster in the places of business where the income is won, it is equally so in the places of living where the income is expended."

A glance at the course of study for the bachelor's degree in the School of Domestic Science will reveal her farsightedness. In addition to chemistry, physics, designing and drawing, British and American authors, German and French classics, political economy, logic, and the history of civilization, one finds household esthetics, mental science, food and dietetics, and home architecture — the last four subjects almost unheard of in 1875, when this plan appeared in print.

When Dr. Gregory gave up his work as Regent of the University in 1880, the position of Professor of Domestic Science was also made vacant, for Miss Allen had become *Mrs.* Gregory! In spite of the promising beginning she had made with the department, the work was allowed to lapse until 1900, when Isabel Bevier arrived to establish a new department with a new name — household science.

In writing of her years as department head Isabel says: "In 1900 under the presidency of Andrew Sloan Draper, when a new order in agriculture was undertaken by Dean Davenport, the suggestion of the education of women was considered, and steps taken to open a department to represent their interest. By that time President Draper had been working hard for six years to overcome what he and Governor Altgeld regarded as the one-sideness of the University.

New Undertakings

"Dean Davenport's efforts toward building up the new college of agriculture had borne fruit in many ways. The most tangible evidence was an appropriation for $150,000 for a new agricultural building. It takes some imagination to visualize the five buildings on the campus when I arrived — the President's house, University Hall, Chemistry, now the Entomology Building, part of the Natural History Building, and the Engineering Building. The appropriation for 1899 was $593,566 and $50,000 interest on endowments. Of these sums, $150,000 for the Agricultural Building and $10,000 for a course of domestic economy are of special interest to us. But these statistics give no idea of the atmosphere of the campus. It was literally buzzing with newness, new buildings, new courses, and new members of the faculty, all of them infused with the spirit of adventure and open-mindedness toward experimentation.

"The list of new undertakings that had followed in the wake of President Draper's arrival included the Music Department, Library and Law Schools. The Chicago Schools of Medicine, Dentistry, and Pharmacy came trooping along. In the words of Alice in Wonderland, 'In my country one must run to keep up.' And into all this newness I came from ten years' experience in teaching chemistry and natural science in women's colleges in Pennsylvania and Ohio and a year's residence in Boston, where I had studied in Massachusetts Institute of Technology with Mrs. Ellen S. Richards and Professor W. T. Sedgwick.

"My enthusiasm for the new chance was checked when

33

I realized in part the size of the venture that I was to undertake in September, especially since I was conscious of my lack of either experience or training in what was then known as domestic science. To be sure, when I was studying chemistry with Professor Albert W. Smith of Case School of Applied Sciences, he had told me that the place for women in chemistry was in food chemistry, and acting upon his suggestion I had studied food chemistry in Massachusetts Institute of Technology and in Professor W. O. Atwater's laboratory. Also I had made it plain to President Draper and Dean Davenport that fine cooking was not in my repertoire, and both Mrs. Richards and Professor Atwater had emphasized the fact that my special training had been in the chemistry of foods and nutrition. Indeed, I learned some years later that Professor Atwater had written definitely to President Draper that if the department was expected to be organized on cooking-school lines, I had better not be called as I would be a misfit, and President Draper had said to me, 'I don't care if you can cook or not, I will get somebody to do that. I want you to run your department and it will be judged by the results obtained in its laboratories and classrooms and its success by the measure of University respect obtained for it.'

Getting Settled

"I devoted considerable time that summer of 1900 to collecting ideas at the Lake Placid Conference which was then, and for many years, the best source of ideas for this new type of work. On September 1, I arrived in Champaign, settled my possessions in two rooms at 802 West Illinois Street and immediately sought conferences with my superior officers.

"President Draper told me to visit the various departments and see what I could find that I wanted to incorporate
in the new department. My pedometer showed that for
three days I had averaged five miles per day in even the
restricted space from the Engineering Building to the top
floor of the Natural History Building, where the department
was temporarily located. The new Agricultural Building,
following the lot of new buildings as I learned afterward,
was not ready for occupancy. Each day was an adventure
into the great unknown. The liabilities of the department
were many. Its assets were chiefly the good will and farsightedness and the genuine interest of those in authority,
assets not to be lightly esteemed.

"The naming of this new educational child was entrusted
by President Draper to Dean Davenport, Vice-President
Burrill, and me, and here Dean Davenport's guiding hand
appeared. The three of us wanted science as the basis and
approach to the subject; but it was Dean Davenport who
said, 'I believe there will be some day a science of the
household. Let's get ready for it and develop it.' So the child
was called 'household science,' and thus due warning was
given that neither a cooking school nor a milliner's shop was
being opened at the University. Immediate plans had to be
made for class instruction. The new laboratory could not be
ready before the second semester, but Dr. Burrill said, 'It
has been advertised all over the state that a new department
is to be opened, so you must teach something.' That was
quite a poser, but I was so anxious not to have the food work
begin until the second semester of the first year that I was
glad to do anything that would help toward that end. The
fact that we could have no laboratory justified our post-
poning it.

Many Men Help

"In my search for ideas and help I went naturally to the Chemistry Department first, because of my experience as a teacher of chemistry, and found Professor A. W. Palmer and Dr. H. S. Grindley most anxious to help. Also Mrs. Richards had told me to go to 'that nice old man in Engineering, Dean Ricker; he is the best of them all.' He was most helpful, and through his influence, as well as that of Professor J. M. White, was established a close connection with the College of Engineering, for many years the only such alliance in the country. That connection enabled us to provide for this wonderful opening course which both Dean Davenport and Vice-President Burrill had said must be given to the freshmen if we wished to build up a strong department. After much thought it was decided that the course formerly given in the College of Engineering, which had included six lectures each on history of architecture, heating, and plumbing, should be moved over, revamped and renamed in the Department of Household Science. Professor White came nobly to the rescue, and we opened a course in home architecture and sanitation. I chose that name because I thought we could teach a greater variety of things about the house and the home under that name than under any other, and I wanted the class to begin early to understand that what we were working at under any and all names was the home.

"Shelter" First

"The Lake Placid Conference had suggested that the work in home economics should center around food, shelter, and clothing, and I chose to begin with shelter so as to have a tangible basis for the work. In household science 2, as we called home architecture and sanitation, Professor

White taught house planning most skillfully. Other members of the engineering staff gave lectures on heating, plumbing, and lighting, while Dean Ricker gave a course in the history of architecture, and I supplied the woman's point of view about the home.

"I still think we planned better than we knew when we made that approach to the subject. Almost daily I went to Dean Davenport to recount my successes and failures and to find out what to do next. You who knew his facility in that direction understand that I was never without a job. There was always in Dean Davenport's mind the broader outlook, the ability to see things in their relationship. These qualities made him a wonderful dean for a department looked upon with suspicion. This thing of putting science into the household was not always kindly received. Even the dean of liberal arts, though kindly disposed, had said, 'How much credit are you asking for bread making?' and I said, 'Not much, because we are not baking much bread.' It was a source of real satisfaction two years later to have that same dean say to me, 'We are making some changes in the catalog in liberal arts and I would like to include two of your courses, home sanitation and home decoration.'

A Course Is Planned

"Dean Davenport always had time to listen, to evaluate, to decide about the time to be spent in courses and the proportion of credit for the whole group. It was decided at the beginning that only about one-quarter of the student's time should be given to household science because of the requirements in science, history, literature and art — all of which we included in our plan for a liberal education for women. A colleague of mine working in Missouri at the same time once said, 'I don't know as I would like to have a dean that knows as much about home economics as Dean Davenport does. I wouldn't know whether it was his course or mine.' I was never troubled that way. I always knew that it was a composite gathered from many people.

"Miss Elizabeth Sprague, mentioned in President Draper's telegram, had been too ill to come, so I was left to open the ball. The annals of the University this time furnish the following data: 'March 13, 1900, Department of Domestic Science established. September, 1900, Organization of the School of Household Science.' The University catalog of 1899-1900 shows architecture, bacteriology, chemistry, economics, and physiology offered under the caption 'Household Economics.' This variety of names shows something of the confusion attending the work.

First Registration

"When registration had ended we found that we had 20 students and three courses, one on architecture and sanitation, for the first semester; the second on selection and preparation of food, and the third on home decoration, for the second semester. Later in the semester we moved into the north wing of the new Agricultural Building and proceeded to plan kitchens and the beginnings of a chemical laboratory. For the one course which I felt really prepared to offer there were no students. I had worked it out when in Massachusetts Institute of Technology, and it had been approved by Mrs. Richards and Professor Sedgwick, and I had taught it at Lake Erie College. It was the chemistry of food and nutrition, but no student had sufficient work in either foods or chemistry to take it.

"I had, however, plenty to do in the course in home

sanitation and in planning the development of the courses listed. Planning the work in foods proved to be a real undertaking. In those days where to begin with food was a great question. Nine land-grant institutions had courses in 'domestic economy' in 1900: Iowa State College, Kansas State Agricultural College, South Dakota State College, Oregon State College, the Agricultural College of Utah, Colorado Agricultural College, Michigan State College, Ohio State University, and Montana State College. But, judged by their catalogs, the work seemed to me to be on the cooking-school basis. The courses were listed as cooking and advanced cooking, including salads, which I had thought were made mostly from raw materials. I sought for another classification and finally decided to use the method I was familiar with in the teaching of chemistry — namely, to take the classes of foods and study one class until the student knew something about it. Proteins, fats, and carbohydrates were the classes we decided to begin with — protein because of its importance and because it would give us the work with meat in midwinter. Cooking seemed to me so inadequate that after much thought I chose 'selection and preparation of food' for the title of the first semester's work in foods and 'economical use of food' for the second semester's work.

A "Home" Room — in 1900!

"For the home-decoration work I begged, bought, and borrowed all manner and kinds of house furnishing materials, from Tiffany vases to six-cent wallpaper, and fitted up a room in the new building to illustrate home furnishings.

"No day passed that some one or ten people did not appear to see the 'noo buildin',' the 'noo' department, and the 'noo' woman, or to find out about something. There were distinguished visitors who wished to have explained how cooking could belong in a university. Teaching classes, planning courses, answering the telephone, and receiving visitors kept me busy.

Operation "Telephone"

"One morning in the early dawn when I was mapping out my day's work, I said to myself, 'It is not fair to my class to have all these interruptions by telephone and visitors. I am going to pay no attention to the telephone.' We were only well started in the class work when the telephone began. Remembering my resolution I kept bravely on, as did also the telephone. Finally I gave up and went to my office to answer it and found Dr. Burrill at the other end of the line saying, 'When we get the new building, what do you think we had better call it? Just the Woman's Building or Gregory Hall, or some other name?' Stalling for time I said, 'Oh, I can't decide on such a big question — let me call you later,' and I went back to my class.

"About two minutes later I heard steps on the stairs. Soon Dean Davenport, accompanied by two gentlemen, passed the door with a nod which seemed to say, 'Your office, please.' I went in to be introduced to the noted Irishman, Sir Horace Plunkett, and to Sir William McDonald, the Governor General of Canada. Needless to say, my resolution not to be interrupted faded in the face of such opposition, but Dean Davenport saw that I needed a secretary and he provided one.

How to Handle Critics

"Critics came too, among them a superintendent who had two daughters in school and who knew exactly what ought to be done about woman's education. At the very sight of him I knew something was the matter. One night after a hard day, as I was leaving the building I met him at the head of the stairs and rather surprised him by saying, 'Well, I am in a hurry, what is the matter? Let's have it now.' He said, 'What do you mean?' And I said, 'There is always something the matter, and I thought we might as well get it over with.' Not exactly a tactful procedure, I admit. He said, 'Do you know you haven't the word cooking in that catalog once?' I was greatly relieved and said, 'Oh, that is because cooking is not all that we do with food. Some we freeze, some we dry, some we just wash and eat raw. I wanted a chance for a large liberty for my work in food so I said "selection and preparation," which covers much more nearly what I want to do.'

"Then there was the man fond of horses. I had spent considerable time and thought on fitting up the hall at the head of the stairs so as to make an attractive reception room, and Professor Wells (teacher of art) and I had been commissioned to go to Chicago to select some pictures and some chairs and a book rack to add to its attractiveness. The pictures were Corot's 'Dance of the Nymphs,' Millet's 'The Gleaners,' and one other of that type. They had been framed, according to the custom then, in rather broad frames. Imagine my surprise to have this man say, 'If you don't look out, the first thing you know you will just have a collection of frames here. Why don't you have a picture of a good horse?' I was amused, but I hesitated a moment and then I said, 'I don't know where I can get a picture of a good horse. Could you get one for me?' He didn't seem so certain that he could produce one.

"Day by day I was acquiring the idea of what the land-grant college meant in education: that it belonged to all the people; that the state university was to serve the interest of the state; that what we found out in our laboratories if helpful was to be passed on. This viewpoint was very different from what I had been accustomed to. I had been associated with the aristocratic idea of education. No responsibility was undertaken for interpreting the common life and the daily tasks on a scientific basis. So far as women's education was concerned at that time, the idea of working on a scientific basis was a very great contribution from the land-grant college. The cooking schools, with their rule-of-thumb methods, could not get very far; but the scientific explanation for the action and reaction of heat, cold, acids, and alkalis opened up a whole new world.

Religion in the Land-Grant College

"Another of my surprises in these early days was the attitude of those in authority toward religion. I came with the idea that land-grant colleges were very godless places and I found each of my superior officers pillars in their respective churches, men not only of high principles but active, outspoken, working Christians, and the student Y. M. C. A. and Y. W. C. A., factors in the social and religious life of the student body. In those early days I think the land-grant college did much for the farm boy and girl, not only in broadening their intellectual horizon but in developing their social life. The contacts in classroom, clubs, churches, Y. M. C. A. and Y. W. C. A. of all the classes and kinds from all the colleges of the University gave the country-bred individual new ideas as to the importance of social gifts, and the town-bred group respect for the substantial qualities of their country cousins.

"A teacher of English, city-bred, said to me, 'I am glad to have the agriculture boys in my classes. They have not read anything and don't know English, but they go to work at it just as they would work at digging ditches. They work intelligently and they soon learn to read discriminately.' A woman who came to my staff from a land-grant institution in the Northwest said, 'The Illinois home economics girls have a very different social status from what I have been accustomed to. The Illinois girls seem to be in the center of the campus social life. Those I knew were segregated.'

"All this was what we called inside work, but many contacts had to be made on the outside. Dean Davenport had me visit three homes which he called typical Illinois homes. Each was on an eight-hundred-acre farm. To be sure, I learned later that not all the Illinois farms had eight hundred acres, but the Raymonds and the Fulkersons whom he selected were leaders in better farming and better living. The Farmers' Institute was already a growing concern, and the women's division, afterward named the Home Science Department, was already at work under the leadership of Mrs. Henry Dunlap, Mrs. Raymond, Mrs. Carter, Mrs. S. Noble King, and others. Through these women, arrangements were made for the School for Housekeepers which was held the last two weeks in January and which brought together women for demonstrations and for discussion of the problems of the home.

"Dean Davenport was interested in having me visit other institutions in which similar work was being conducted. So I went to places as widely separated as McDonald Institute in Canada, the Detroit Manual Training School, the Philadelphia Museum. I spoke at Farmers' Institutes, at the educational meeting of Canadians at Toronto, and made my debut at the annual meeting of the Farmers' Institute at Jacksonville, Illinois, in February of my first year. Mrs. Carriel, the daughter of Johnathan B. Turner of land-grant fame, told me years afterward that I turned to her as I sat on the platform trembling and said, 'If I had known that this kind of thing went with my job, I would never have accepted the position.'

Household Science Defined

"The following excerpt from the address given at Jacksonville will show something of what we were attempting:

" 'We come now to consider the second question, what do you mean by household science? Youmans has said it includes a study of the agents, the material, and the phenomena of the household. We need to pause a moment and repeat the words to appreciate the largeness of the suggestion. The agents, heat, light, food, electricity, cold; the materials, the air we breathe, the food we eat, the water we drink, the houses we live in. Who will complete the list? It is well to remember that principles are universal, while the applications are special and particular. The general laws of heat are as true for the modern range as for the steam engine. The painter, the decorator, and the dyer have a technical interest in color, but the woman who would give beauty and personality to her home by a harmonious blending of color cannot disregard these same principles that govern the technical work. Women have been rather slow to recognize the close relation science sustains to the affairs of the home; and, by some strange oversight, provision has not been made for them to apply science in fields particularly their own. Is there any good reason why the girl should not apply her knowledge of chemistry to bread and of bacteriology to the processes of fermentation? I believe it is our privilege to benefit by the educational experiments conducted on the men. They have tested successively the classical school, the manual training school, the technical school; and our universities stand today because men have found that the widest development, the truest unfolding, of the human spirit was to be accomplished, not by any one of the schools, but by the correlation of the best elements of each.

" 'This brings us directly to our last topic, the position of household science in a state university. I answer: to provide a place and an opportunity for the correlation and application of the arts and sciences to the home. I know of no one place which affords so many opportunities for these applications. Neither do I know of a place more fateful for good or evil in the life of the individual or the nation than the home. As the equipment and advantages of the University greatly exceed those of any single college, so are the opportunities for the household science department greatly multiplied. . . .

" 'The College of Science can reveal to the students some of the mysteries of the laws of life. The College of Liberal Arts can give them a better conception of their own place and work in the world by the study of the history and literature of other peoples and tongues. The eye can be trained to recognize beauty of color and outline, and the hand to express it in constructing and adorning the house beautiful. A wise selection and correlation of work in these various lines, combined with the experienced work of the Household Science Department, affords an unusual opportunity for that symmetrical development so greatly to be desired in educational training.'

"One other outstanding event so far as agriculture and household science were concerned in that first year was the dedication of our new Agricultural Building. With the interest centered in agriculture, we had to put our best foot forward to show our part in the new building: namely, the north wing over the dairy. By that time we had a kitchen, an office, part of a chemistry laboratory, two classrooms, and illustrative material of various kinds. There were many distinguished guests. We were especially interested in Miss Alice M. Ravenhill, who was sent to the United States by the English government to study the work of household science in the United States. Her own work in London had made its approach through hygiene. We found her a most interesting and stimulating woman, and afterward we read with admiration the report of her visit to the United States because of her understanding of the movement as a whole.

"President Draper had said to me, 'I don't care very much about your running around the country for the farmers' institutes. I doubt if you have the time to give to them, but I do feel that you ought to go to the state meetings like the Federation of Women's Clubs and the educational meeting at Springfield.' So for ten years I went regularly to represent the University at the meeting of the Federation of Women's Clubs and told them of our plans and our problems.

Isabel and the Trustees

"In my early days I wasn't particularly enthusiastic over the women trustees of the University. They seemed not to understand what we were trying to do nor to be very much interested in it. During the first semester Miss Cornelia Simon had been added to the staff, and word had reached us that the trustees were to meet at the University. Miss Simon was much surprised when she said to me, 'I suppose the women trustees will come here first,' and I said, 'I doubt it — they usually go to the cattle barns and don't have time to get here.' I do not wish to seem unappreciative of the women trustees, for after the first few years we spoke the same language and understood each other.

Extract from Catalog, 1901-1902

"The following extract from the catalog of 1901-1902 tells something of the idea back of the work:

"'The Household Science Department of the University of Illinois is one of the new departments, being only a little more than a year old. Its position among the departments is somewhat unique because of the correlation of its work with the offerings of other colleges. The introduction of a Department of Household Science into our colleges and universities is substantial evidence of a change of ideals in education, particularly in the education of women. . . . Social and industrial forces have made themselves felt in the curricula of our colleges and universities. The Household Science Department of the University of Illinois may be said to put the emphasis upon three things: First, a symmetrical education upon a scientific basis. There is no necessity to plead now for the recognition of the claims of science. Its contributions to the sum of human knowledge give it first rank among the benefactors of mankind. The accuracy, thoroughness, and breadth of mental vision which its study justifies are most desirable mental attributes.

" 'Second, it emphasizes the benefits of applied science for women. This is in a sense a departure from the traditions of the fathers, more particularly from those of the mothers.

" 'Third, the Household Science Department asks for the recognition of the home in the education of women, it being the one place to which the energy of most of them is directed. Women are everywhere members of a household; their health, their comfort, and their efficiency oftentimes depend upon a knowledge of household processes and the science which underlies them.'

"The following data are summarized from the catalog:

"1900-1901. Miss Bevier and Miss Simon: selection and preparation of food, home sanitation, elementary home decoration, chemistry and nutrition of food, dietetics.

"1901-1902. Miss Beatty and Miss Bevier: selection and preparation of food, home architecture and sanitation, elementary home decoration, chemistry of food and nutrition, dietetics and household management, economic uses of food, textiles, personal and public hygiene, seminar.

"The same courses were offered in 1902-03 and in 1903-04. In 1904-05 there were ten courses and two graduate courses. The enrollment reads: first year 20, second year 40, third year 60, fourth year 80.

"1903 is the most important date because in that year the Legislature passed the bill appropriating $80,000 for a new woman's building. Much credit for this is due to the persistence and wise efforts of Senator and Mrs. Henry Dunlap.

"The first class was graduated in 1903: Miss Ellen Huntington, Miss Mabel Nelson, and Miss Ruth A. Wardall. That was really a great event, and no less a person than President Van Hise of the University of Wisconsin came to see the Department and asked particularly that he might see what manner of women were seniors. In 1904 there were four graduates, and in 1905, five. 1904 marked our beginning of graduate work with the addition of Miss Susannah Usher.

"I have given in considerable detail the work of the opening years in order to give a better understanding of the status of household science at the University of Illinois. There were no precedents to follow, many rocks to be avoided, many people to be pleased, but through it all I had the support of those in authority and much satisfaction in developing a new work. It was a real source of regret to me when President Draper left to take up his work as Commissioner of Education in New York State. He had been such a tower of strength to me, considerate and helpful in many unexpected ways, so appreciative of the difficulties and of my efforts.

Moving Into the Woman's Building

"The growth in number of students of agriculture and household science made necessary a change in location for the Household Science Department. The north wing of the beautiful new Woman's Building was its next home. The appropriation of $80,000 had been increased by $15,000 and on January 26, 1904, the plans of McKim, Meade, and White of New York were presented and adopted. The plan was U-shaped, 194 feet 8 inches by 83 feet 6 inches, the central section being planned as a women's gymnasium, the north wing for the Household Science Department, and the South wing for social headquarters for women.

"On October 16, 1905, the dedicatory service took place in the gymnasium of the new building as one of the features of the installation of President Edmund Janes James. The principal speakers were President James and President Lilian W. Johnson of the Western College for Women in Oxford, Ohio. The first classes were held in the new Woman's Building on November 7, 1905. The additional space provided opportunity for much better working conditions, called for new equipment, also provided space for the School for Housekeepers held each January, a group which had grown in numbers from thirty to one hundred seventy-five. Each succeeding year saw additions to the student body as well as to the staff. The demand for speakers at the Farmers' Institute increased. A syllabus was made for the high schools. A woman was added to the staff to help them, and special thought was given to providing for teachers in the summer work. Emphasis was put upon the development of the art side of the work, as told in the following statement issued at that time:

Advancing in Applied Arts

"'Perhaps our most noteworthy advance has been along applied arts. Those who have investigated the subjects of textile and domestic art in our colleges and universities realize what a heterogenous collection is included under that title. Much of it judged by educational, economic, or esthetic standards is of little value. Everyone recognizes the desirability of educating women to be intelligent consumers of the commodities that form so large a part of their own

49

possessions and are so important in furnishing their homes. It has been, however, a work of much time and patience to select from the data offered those elements which ought to form a part of the University courses in textiles, together with those processes of applied art which most directly concern the woman in the home. Miss Charlotte Gibbs has given hours to this problem with skill, and the results of her efforts, as shown in our new course in household art, seem to me most worthy of commendation. In this connection I would like to say that whatever may be done to strengthen the university offerings along the line of art and design will be of great benefit to the work of the Department of Household Science.'

The New President — Edmund James

"I had dreaded the change of presidency. President Draper and I had understood each other from the first, and I had always found it easy to talk over my plans with him. A rumor obtained on the campus that President James had the German conception of woman's place and work and was not in sympathy with women in University pursuits. I felt that that attitude would make it difficult for me, especially in the development of new policies. I was obligated to consult with the president frequently. However, he seemed businesslike and agreeable and my feelings were relieved. My testing time came very unexpectedly. I had gone over to see President James on a rather minor matter. In the midst of our conversation he turned to me and said in his quick, abrupt way, 'Now, Miss Bevier, you know your groups are not made up of college students. Oh, you may have a few, but most of them are specials and irregulars.' To have this said to me after I had really battled for ten years to have chemistry as a requirement for admission to our work and had offended some of those in high places by my insistence was too much to stand. I answered quickly and with considerable feeling, 'President James, you are mistaken. Our group is made up of college students. We have very few specials. I can't give you figures now, but I can send them to your office within an hour.' 'All right, get them over here,' was the reply, and I hurried back to my office. The data were collected hastily, and to my joy our proportion of special students was less than that given by the Registrar for the University as a whole. I sent the data and called attention to the fact.

"I came to have great admiration for President James personally and his manner of doing things. He was sometimes abrupt, but you could be too. He would listen to you respectfully and tell you what he thought of the procedure. He was so impersonal. The subject of discussion was either for or against the good of the University and stood or fell by that standard. But you had your chance. If you could give a good reason for your request and there was money available, it was granted. If you had not thought it through carefully it were wiser to stay away until you had. In any case the chapter was closed, with no disagreeable hangover because of a difference of opinion. You could do an immense amount of business with him in five minutes if you were ready to answer his question, 'What is on your mind and heart today? — one, two, three.' Then the end, 'All right, go ahead,' and he sent you out of his office with new courage.

Innovation in Research

"In 1908 two new ventures were undertaken. So many questions were being asked in the classrooms and over the state about the daily processes and products of the home that the necessity for research work had long been evident. The Department was fortunate in securing the service of

Miss Nellie E. Goldthwaite, A.M., Ph.D., who had been for several years head of the Department of Chemistry at Mt. Holyoke College and later was research assistant in the Rockefeller Institute of Medical Research. Incidentally, it may be added that Miss Goldthwaite was the first woman secured by a department of Home Economics for research work alone. She did outstanding work, finding the answer to the question what makes jelly jell, and also the solutions to many problems regarding bread. Also she was in charge of the graduate students.

The Experimental House

"The second venture was the securing of an experimental house. This house, at the corner of Wright and Daniel near the Woman's Building, provided an unusual opportunity for working at the problems of a home. It served as a laboratory for most of the classes. The classes in house planning, furnishing, and decoration derived the most benefit because of the improvements that had to be made. Doors and windows were changed, the kitchen made lighter, and the whole question of furniture and furnishings was studied. Part of the furnishings were bought in Chicago, part were generously lent by local dealers.

"In addition the house served as a laboratory for the community; as many as 80 visitors came in one day to see not only the furniture, but the new electric equipment. Wide publicity was given to it by visitors and reporters from Chicago and St. Louis.

"In 1910 I was granted a much-needed leave of absence. I spent part of the month of September in Boston and visited various kinds of schools. On October 1, through the courtesy and generosity of Professor Chittenden and Dr. Mendel of

Yale, I went to Dr. Mendel's laboratory, where for two months I had the privilege of working and of seeing this great teacher at work. Then I moved on to New York City, with Columbia University as my immediate goal. Here again I was given opportunity to visit classes, observe laboratory work, and go on numerous excursions ranging from Campbell's soup plant to Tiffany's glass works. It was a real privilege. Later I visited schools in the South — notably Miss Berry's at Rome, Georgia — in Pittsburgh, in Ohio, and in various parts of the Middle West. I improved my opportunity to collect ideas in regard to education.

Trouble Brews

"Meanwhile the age-old conflict between the cooking and sewing school adherents and those who believed in the scientific method of approach to the teaching of household science had gone on in the Farmers' Institute circle.

"My insistence on university standards for entrance had not found favor in all quarters, particularly since the boys were admitted to the College of Agriculture on easier terms. It was no comfort to the dissenters that a representative of the Carnegie Foundation rated the Department of Household Science as the only one of college rank in the College of Agriculture.

"This opposition found expression in a resolution by the household science department of the Farmers' Institute voicing its disapproval of our department. Possibly if I had not been so busy developing the department, speaking at Farmers' Institutes and writing texts to use in the department, and had had the patience and taken the time to seek the favor of these women, the breach might have been avoided.

"The final straw was my refusal to accept the proposition to work for an appropriation which the insurgents felt certain could be secured if I would agree to an advisory committee of their number to work for me for the department. I already had as advisers the deans of the three colleges in which the department gave courses and the President of the University. Since those women and I had never spoken the same language and held such opposite ideas about the teaching of household science, I could not expect help from such a committee. I was warned by Dean Davenport if I refused this offer, I must do it at my own risk. I said, 'I take the risk.'

Asked to Resign

"Dean Davenport honestly felt that the good of the department would be served by my resignation and wrote urging me to resign. Fortunately for all concerned I was in Columbia as an observer when the letter came. At that distance I could have a better perspective and not trouble my friends at the University. President James and Dean David Kinley were most considerate and helpful, but after all the decision as to my return rested with me. I was assured by them that the way was open for me to return if I wished to do so. After much consideration I decided to ask advice from my good friend, former President Draper. I knew he understood the situation. I had faith in his judgment, and it was a real comfort to have the counsel of so wise a friend.

An Old Friend's Advice . . .

"President Draper investigated and found that the opposition was all outside of the University. He said to me, 'If you leave now you can spend the rest of your life telling why you left the University of Illinois. Go back and tend strictly to your own business and I think you will be supported.'

. . . Leads to the Right Choice

"So in July I returned. President James and Dean Kinley, then Vice-President and Dean of the Graduate School, had through it all given me their cordial support and welcomed me back. In deference to the wishes of the opposition, the experimental house had been given up in my absence, but the enrollment grew. I was warmly welcomed by my colleagues and by my staff. In the spring of 1911 the General Assembly granted our request for an addition to our Woman's Building in order that we might more adequately serve the needs of the women. I may add that later Dean Davenport came to me and said, 'You were right and I was wrong. I greatly overestimated the strength of the opposition.' So there was restored the old working relations, and the friendship of many years was strengthened.

Pillars or "Pile-ons"?

"Time went quickly, the enrollment of the University grew rapidly. We had hardly adjusted ourselves to the new Woman's Building, it seemed, before we discovered it was too small and plans for enlarging it were considered. Some of us were very loath to see our beautiful colonial architecture spoiled, much as we wished the space for development. We were fearful that the state architect would not be careful about architectural harmony. I remember very distinctly a conference with President James in which I objected to the pillars at the front entrance. 'For heavens sake, don't call them pillars,' said President James. 'The state architect nearly had a fit when the trustees called them pillars.' 'What are they?' I asked. 'Pylons.' 'Never anything better named,' I said. 'The whole addition is a pile on.'

Additions of All Kinds

"By dint of much labor and thought on the part of Supervising Architect James M. White, an addition two hundred feet in length and forty feet in width was made to the front of the building. The catalog spoke of the new addition as three stories high 'in a free, modern, colonial style with an additional two-story colonnade between the main entrance,' and pylons were forgotten.

"The main divisions of work in the new building as a whole were maintained. Household science still kept the north wing; physical education, the center; the office of the Dean of Women, and the rest rooms for students, and the upper parlors for social events were in the south wing. For household science a new kitchen and dining room were added in the basement. On the second floor a diet kitchen and a room for electrical equipment were enlarged from what already existed. But the great gain for household science came in two outstanding new undertakings: a cafeteria and a practice apartment. The former provided opportunity for training in institutional work with food, while the practice apartment was an evolution of the former experimental house. The cafeteria served the college community and set standards in food. In the apartment the individual student investigated some of the problems of the home, serving as cook for a group of six one week and in succeeding weeks taking on other tasks as her share in the division of labor.

"The informal opening of the new addition on April 25,

1913, was marked by a luncheon for members of the University Senate served in the new cafeteria.

"The work of my department seemed to me always a series of new undertakings and for that reason interesting. A change of location had occurred every five years, with all the attendant opportunities for improvement. While the front was being added to the Woman's Building, it was my daily practice to look over the building to prevent some wrong move by plumbers, carpenters, or painters. One day when there had been no moment to leave my office until almost six, I said to myself, 'I have not gone over the building, but I will let it go now until morning and begin with that walk.' Imagine my dismay at finding nine doors finished in the wrong color. The supervising architect's office, the painter, and the committee on color had to be called and some quick work done.

"Again it had taken a good deal of pressure on my part to get the practice apartment made out of the third-floor waste space. President James said, 'You won't like it when you get it.' 'Why won't I?' I said. 'Because the windows will have to be in the corners and the whole space is a queer shape.' I said, 'There is much more space in it than some Chicago families live in. I think it is the business of the architect to make a livable apartment out of that much space.' And we were all rather proud of the attractive five-room-and-bath apartment that was made and abides to this day [1934] in active use. Moreover, and still more strange, some of the furnishings bought in 1908 for the experimental house are in use in the practice apartment in 1934.

"The Things That Are Fixed Are Dead"

"Just as all seemed to be going well with the apartment,

a call came from the President's office. When I arrived, President James said, 'You can't have that pantry up there with all those wooden shelves. That is supposed to be a fireproof building.' I said, 'There are a good many places that will burn before fire reaches to the third floor.' So though everybody really wished to be helpful, it was not easy to make plans and to watch over carpenters, plumbers, and painters. I learned to count it as part of the day's work, but in the beginning it disturbed me a great deal and I said once to Mrs. Richards, 'If only we could get a few things fixed and have them stay fixed.' Mrs. Richards' reply I have many times recalled, 'My child, the things that are fixed are dead.'

"Along with this newness went always my effort to unify the teaching and to keep the balance among the varying demands, in order not to put too much emphasis upon the chemistry of food and forget to teach how to prepare really good food. The development of the art side must be looked after as well as the growing tendency for a better understanding of the economic phases. We found it very difficult to find a woman trained in economics who knew home economics and could relate the two fields properly. Emphasis was being placed upon home and family life and the rights of the children by the formation of the government's Children's Bureau. The question of a child in the practice house had to be considered.

"A step that touched household science most closely was the passage of the Smith-Lever Act* in 1914. The haphazard, politically dominated work of the Farmers' Institute, well-intentioned but uneducational, was over. Their misguided efforts were to be transferred to non-political organizations, directed by men and women trained in educational methods. Not that the Farmers' Institute must be done away with, but that much of its work would be done by government organizations and on a very different basis. I have no intention of discrediting the work done by men and women in Illinois under Farmers' Institute organization. They made ready the soil and many of them gave excellent service, but in the very nature of things the movement was bound to grow into something bigger and better.

Extension Work Begins

"The first effect upon our department was the addition of a woman to serve as our extension worker throughout the state. Miss Mamie Bunch, a graduate of our department, who had formerly been a county superintendent of schools, was chosen for this position and did valiant service in the new work. Miss Bunch and I had many conferences about the method of organization for this new enterprise. We had seen how the women had been handicapped in their efforts for leadership as a department of the Farmers' Institute. Little opportunity was given for them to take the initiative. The most of the plans were made and executed by the men. In those days, women were very timid, afraid of the sound of their own voice in a public audience. They found difficulty in seconding a motion to say nothing of the fear and labor of putting one.

"Miss Bunch and I felt strongly that a special organization 'manned' by women and managed entirely by them might move more slowly but it would offer much better

---

*This act made provision for "cooperative agricultural extension work which shall consist of giving instruction and practical demonstrations in agriculture and home economics to persons not attending nor resident in the agricultural college." It is here that the term *home economics* appears for the first time in federal legislation.

opportunity for women to state their plans and work for their women's meetings, and in so doing develop themselves. We were helped in a very unexpected way in carrying out this decision. The women of Kankakee county wished to organize. They said very frankly they were not willing to be a part of the farm bureau organization; that it was quite impossible for them to work with the man who was then county agent because of his attitude, that while he pretended to favor their organization, in reality he was secretly working against them because he was jealous of their possible power.

"Then we were ready to talk to Dean Davenport and with Mr. Walter Handschin, who was in direct charge of the men's extension work, as I was of the women's, both under Dean Davenport. I have recalled many times the long conference Dean Mann of Cornell, Mr. Handschin, Miss Bunch, and I had about the organization question. As a result, Miss Eva Bennefield, one of our graduates, began work as home adviser in Kankakee county in the new organization of women in October, 1914, and so headed for Illinois that long procession of women home advisers who have worked so well with such steadfast courage and unselfish devotion in the cause of home betterment. It was a real satisfaction to me to have Mr. Handschin say about a year later, 'I was not at all certain about your plan of organization, but I have watched it. I am for it.' The years have proved that the Kankakee women did well for their kind, and the Illinois plan is recognized as superior to the form of organization in many other states. I have sometimes wondered whether the resemblance between the New York and Illinois plans was not born in, or very closely associated with, that conference with Director Mann.

Smith-Hughes Act, 1917

"Extension work on the new foundation was only fairly started when another responsibility was added to our department by the passage of the Smith-Hughes Act in February 1917. Smith-Lever had to do with the field outside, but Smith-Hughes affected the work on the inside, particularly in the training of teachers of vocational education. For us that meant the training of teachers in home economics.

"The purpose of this act was to promote vocational education in agriculture, home economics, trades, and industry, and to provide for the training of teachers in these subjects. Home economics education was defined as that form of vocational education which has for its purpose the preparation of girls and women for useful employment as homemakers engaged in the management of the home. As a result of these two acts, Smith-Lever and Smith-Hughes, and in order to avoid confusion in terms, the name of our department was changed from that of household science to *home economics*.

World War I

"In 1917 the Department of Home Economics had to meet another emergency. The war clouds which had darkened the lands across the sea grew more threatening. The United States planned to enter, and the call to arms for men by President Wilson was quickly followed by a call to the men and women of the country to serve in the first line of defense at home. The University aided the work in every way possible. The newly finished residence hall for women was converted into a barracks for the prospective soldiers. It was suggested that the Woman's Building might be needed for that service.

"Because of the importance of food to the soldier and private citizen as well, agriculture and home economics worked together to meet the nation's needs. Women trained in home economics demonstrated at home the conservation of food by the use of substitutes; while in the hospitals abroad they worked against fearful odds to give food to the soldiers. At least three of our staff went abroad, Miss Ada Hunt and Miss Mary DeGarmo as dietitians and Miss Fannie Brooks as nurse, while many of our girls served in the base hospitals on this side.

"The Food Administrator called women into service from Washington to the remotest country hamlets. In common with most of the heads of departments of home economics in state universities, I was made chairman of the committee for the conservation of food in the Council of National Defense in Illinois, and in addition I served in the office of the Food Administrator in Washington for the months of November and December, 1917.

"Meanwhile the new extension service was greatly increased by workers called in to demonstrate throughout the state how to save wheat and meats. The Home Economics Department offered, in connection with the Animal Husbandry Department, a course on the selection and preparation of cuts of meat. A home-nursing course in charge of a regular trained nurse was another of the offerings of the department. Conservation leaflets on ways to save wheat and meat by the use of substitutes were written by members of the department. The departments of home economics in Milliken, Chicago, and the University of Illinois cooperated in a great food show in the Coliseum in Chicago. Home economists the country over met this emergency well and proved that they had a knowledge of food and could and did render a real service. By the end of the war home economics had earned growing respect from the public.

It was Isabel's custom to write an annual letter to the alumnae of her department. The following gives an idea of the content and spirit of these letters.

UNIVERSITY OF ILLINOIS
Department of Household Science
Urbana, Illinois

bel Bevier, Director
ra E. Gray, Household Management.
th Wheeler, Nutrition
ud E. Parsons, Lunch Room Manage.
orgia E. Fleming, Clothing
rene Seymour, Textiles
rence Harrison, Practice Teaching
na W. Williams, Household Manage.
ona Hope, Costume Design
inda Perry, Economics
ry C. DeGarmo, Dietetics
cile Wheeler, Foods.

Jean G. MacKinnon, Foods
Marie E. Freeman, Lunch Room
Viola J. Anderson, Foods.
Bessie E. Packard, Office Assistant

EXTENSION
Mamie Bunch, State Leader
Olive B. Percival, Demonstration Car
Fannie M. Brooks, Home Nursing
Naomi O. Newburn, Assistant
Anne I. Green, Assistant
Floyd E. Fogle, Demonstration Car

April 30, 1917

Dear Household Science Girls,

It occurred to me that I might follow the example of the multitude and depart from the custom of sending the annual letter and offer as an excuse that I had gone to war. On the other hand, we have made considerable effort to remind people that they could best serve their country by doing their daily tasks until some other was thrust upon them, so I am sending the letter.

It has been an unusual year for us all, I am sure. The whole world seems going somewhere though we do not know where. Our girls, it seems to me, have been much less hysterical than our boys. Many of the latter have departed, part of them to farm in Canada or South Dakota or some other place. I believe it is the verdict of the authorities that three-fourths of them are really serving their families or their nation, and about one-fourth are slackers. Doubtless you know of Dean Davenport's scheme for mobilizing the food resources. His plan has found very general acceptance. Dean Kinley spent a week in Washington, taking with him the bill and staying until he was satisfied that Medill McCormick was to introduce it, so Illinois is really in it.

The University is offering hospital service as outlined in the Red

63

Cross requirements, though the scheme has not yet been accepted by the Red Cross. One hundred and forty-one girls are registered in it, about four-fifths of them taking the three courses, First Aid, Home Nursing, and Surgical Supplies and about thirty taking in addition the courses in Dietetics and Field Problems. Fannie Brooks is working at it from seven in the morning until nine at night, and Miss Ruth Wheeler and Miss DeGarmo are giving the Dietetics. I believe I am to contribute words on the planning of meals, this being in the Field Work course.

I think the Department has seemed somewhat phlegmatic because we have neither thundered nor lightninged, but we have done considerable in the way of getting word to the papers as to what to do with asparagus and rhubarb, and the Extension Division is to follow it up as other fruits and vegetables appear. The regulars are to publish meals and menus giving calorific value and actual meals eaten in the apartment or in the cafeteria.

It seemed for a time as though one could not walk the streets without being held up for something. The University faculty raised $6000 for Belgian relief, and the students, something like $3500, which amount was duplicated by a Chicago friend, so that about $13000 was raised altogether. At present we are equipping an ambulance corps to go to France, so you see several things are doing.

Our six new women proved to be treasures and have risen up to their jobs very satisfactorily. Since they came from Kansas, Minnesota, Simmons, Georgia, and Illinois, it did mean some effort on their part, and I appreciate greatly the way in which they have met the situation.

We are quite happy over the new course which is to be offered in Interior Decoration. Professor Provine of the Department of Architecture is the one who has really pushed it, and contributes of his men for the larger part of the work in the first two years. Miss Hope does a large part of the work in the second two years, with Miss Fleming working in Household Science 2. It is a union of the art side of our work with the courses in architecture, freehand drawing, and landscape design, so that it does make a very good connection between engineering and agriculture.

Omicron Nu and Household Science Club rose up to their privileges and made eighty-five dollars to contribute to the Richards Memorial Fund.

Doubtless all of you are interested in knowing about the celebration of the Fiftieth Anniversary of the Founding of the University. I believe the dates are October 17, 18 and 19, 1918. It seems likely that there will be a great gathering of the clans at that time. The committees have been at work for some time. I am wondering if Household Science ought not to have some special hour even though it could not be either a silver wedding or a crystal one.

On behalf of Miss Packard, (Miss Bevier's secretary) I am saying that it would help her greatly in keeping the records and getting the annual letter to you if you would keep us better informed in regard to changes in your occupation, address, and name. Of course, changes in name are of special interest.

With cordial good wishes for each and every one,

Sincerely

"When the armistice had been signed and the various home economics workers returned to their work, they found some inevitable effects of the war, upon themselves and upon their work. They were very tired, but in the experience they had acquired a wider vision of the world's needs. Progress had stopped within the department because the workers had been called from classrooms and laboratories. Research had been abandoned for the same reason. Meanwhile there was an awakening of interest — people were asking many questions about food. The war experience had taught the layman the close relationship between food and health. Questions of all sorts about processes and products of several kinds cried aloud for research. The National Research Council gave home economics a place in its deliberations, and I was made a member of a subcommittee of the council on food and nutrition. Another result of the war was the opening of new lines of work for women trained in home economics. Dietitians were asked for, not only by hospitals but also by hotels. The banks wanted women trained in home economics to help their clients in thrift programs aimed at wise choice of foods.

"In 1918 another emergency came to the department. A flu epidemic broke out in the University. One morning I met G. Huff on the street and he said to me, 'Miss Bevier, the boys are dying like flies.' All the hospital resources were overtaxed. That afternoon Mr. Huff and Dean T. A. Clark appeared in the Woman's Building to ask that the Woman's gym be used as a hospital for women. I was somewhat appalled by this undertaking because being such a well person I had never been a patient in any hospital and knew very little about them, but I said we would do what we could. All the women on the University staff responded most generously in support of the project. By night three patients arrived. Nurses were called from Danville to take care of them because the local supply was exhausted. Some of the staff attended to the sterilization of dishes; others who had nursing experience offered their services to care for the patients. Fortunately no one died, although I never saw such a fight for life as one nurse put up with a patient. At ten o'clock I said to the nurse, 'That woman is dying — her face shows it now.' 'Oh, I know it,' the nurse said, but for four hours she waged her battle and at 2 a.m. we could see a decided change. She turned to me and said, 'You can go home. She won't die tonight,' and I went with unbounded admiration for that nurse as a life saver.

Resignation, 1921

"By 1920 I saw very clearly the need for a new building for home economics. I felt that I did not want to go through all the work of planning and overseeing it and by the time it was completed leave it to my successor who might not approve of my plans. Moreover, President James' health had failed and he was going. Dean Davenport was approaching the retiring age. Life looked very difficult for me, and I was physically very much exhausted. It seemed wiser in the interest of the department and my own health to resign and I did against the protest of many people. At the urgent request of both Dean Davenport and President Kinley, I agreed to take a leave of absence from June to October and return with the understanding that with no more words I would be allowed to leave in June of 1921, which I did."

It was characteristic of Isabel Bevier that when she felt she had built an enduring institution and guided it through the most vigorous years of her life she was willing to leave it to others for future development.

In the words of Dean Davenport, "She put her life, her strength, and her all into her work and her 'girls.' After twenty years she was weary, and against the wishes of all of us she laid down the work for a much needed rest."

One ceremony marked her resignation: that was the formal presentation of her portrait to the University. The high esteem in which Miss Bevier and her work were held on her own campus is shown in the following excerpts from the address given at this time by Dean Davenport on home economics at Illinois:

Dean Davenport's Farewell

"Whatever the name [household science or home economics] the subject matter of study covers these three great fundamentals of civilized society — food, clothing, and shelter. Chemistry having been a leading science in this field, as in agriculture, it was quite necessary to employ this great science in the earliest stages of exploration; but it became more and more evident that not only chemistry but physics and physiology lay at the bottom of the food question, if not also of clothing. Later on, the subject of expending family income began to bulk large in the study and teaching of this subject. Finally, this department has never for a moment forgotten the fact that all these subjects are distinctly humanistic and involve to an exceptional degree that quality known as the human equation.

"From the very first the department has been keenly

conscious of its objective. It has constantly kept in mind the thought of human beings in the home relation, and its great purpose has always been to improve the home, either directly through the training of housekeepers or indirectly through the training of teachers.

"It is my abiding opinion that this fact lies very close to the foundation of the remarkable success that has attended the career of Professor Bevier in the University of Illinois. The one purpose always in mind as the final goal of all that might be said and done and taught was nothing less than the American home. For her ability to keep this in mind amid all the stress and strain of pioneer endeavor, the country owes her a debt of gratitude above that which is owing to most women.

"If efforts are to be judged by their results, it is not too much to say that the purposes of this department have been in the main accomplished, by which is meant that the department has trained hundreds of competent executives and teachers without such exclusive attention to the professional as to break the contact with that great mass of university women who are to become, not teachers or professionals of any kind, but the heads of American homes. To achieve this double purpose has been the great ambition of the department, in which it has eminently succeeded.

"Naturally, when a great work has been accomplished, we seek the individual whose leadership has blazed the way. In this case the individual was not hard to find.

"Professor Bevier has given her life unsparingly to the development of this department. The field was almost entirely new as a university subject. There was naturally much impatience twenty years ago at what appeared to be slow progress. There was much demand for the doing of impossible things, and here, as in many cases, it was the friends of the movement who in some respects made progress difficult by expecting of the department what it could not render without entirely setting aside its university objective.

"If it had yielded to pressure fifteen or twenty years ago, we should not have, as we do now, strong and well-developed departments of home economics in hundreds of high schools in the country. Realizing the significance of a university department in home economics, Professor Bevier set her face strenuously to the development of such courses of instruction as would produce permanent results.

"It was decidedly pioneer work for Professor Bevier and her co-laborers. In other places other pioneers were dreaming and working, but each was practically working alone, for the study was not understood in university circles, even being considered in many places an academic joke.

"In many ways these good women did not have even a fair chance. For example, when a well-trained professor is greeted in the morning by her associates with the threadbare question, 'Have you got the dishes washed?' it is not the sort of inspiration needed to develop a great new subject. By attending strictly to its business and by getting results, this department has slowly but surely justified itself, not only in the opinion of the student body and of the public, but of the faculty as well.

"I think it is not too much to say that at present no department of the University enjoys more of the confidence and respect of the institution than does the department of home economics. To say that this gratifying achievement is mainly the work of one person is perhaps putting it too strongly because Professor Bevier has many able and loyal associates. But even so, the difficult task of choosing between alternative courses, of deciding what to do and what not to do, what to undertake and what to let alone — this great task has rested almost entirely with the head of the department. Her nearest associates in administrative circles have been obliged to rest content with standing on the side lines, dropping here and there a word of encouragement but realizing all the time that their real service was of slight account. All in all, therefore, whatever success we have achieved in this University in the development of home economics must go, so far as leadership is concerned, exclusively to the one whom we honor today.

"She has not only been a force in the development of her chosen subject in the University of Illinois, but she has been a national figure as well. She has been an inspiration to thousands of young women who have been so fortunate as to come under her influence, and she has been a benediction to the University.

"We count it fortunate for those who may come and go as the years go by, and fortunate for those who sojourn here that so excellent a portrait of so lovely a character shall be left among us as almost a speaking remembrance of one who so long labored that others might live better lives."

Chapter III

Beyond the Classroom

Isabel Bevier's broad interpretation of home economics extended beyond her classroom and beyond the campus of the University of Illinois. During the time she served as department head, she wrote books and articles, addressed a variety of audiences, and was prominent in state and national organizations. Her personality and her ideas were of lasting influence in shaping the American Home Economics Association and in giving direction to the whole home economics movement. The strength of her influence is reflected in the statement made by Dr. H. C. Sherman when he said that the scientific esteem in which home economics is held in any comparable institution is closely proportional to the fidelity with which it has followed the standard set by Isabel Bevier.

The American Home Economics Association, incorporated in 1909, grew out of conferences held annually from 1899 to 1909 at the Lake Placid (N.Y.) Club upon the invitation of Mr. and Mrs. Melvil Dewey. Before coming to the University of Illinois in 1900, Isabel Bevier attended the second of these conferences which were, as she said, "then and for many years after the best source of ideas" in home economics. She continued to attend almost all of the conferences and as officer, committee member, and participant in discussion she contributed her enthusiasm, and her ideals and ideas as well as her plans for making them effective. Not all the conference members sympathized with her point of view, but one needs only to give a superficial examination to the papers she read and to the reports from the meetings to realize that she built into the organization a combination of common sense and academic insight rarely found.

The first conference was attended by only eleven persons, with Ellen Swallow Richards as chairman and Melvil Dewey as secretary. Not even the most forward-looking of the eleven realized that they were launching an idea which within fifty years would develop into an organization of some twenty thousand members with a salaried staff and a good-sized office building of its own in Washington, D.C.

At the second meeting Isabel was appointed a member of a committee on courses of study in universities, with Mrs. Mary Roberts of Leland Stanford University as chairman. In 1901 she was herself chairman of a committee on nomenclature and also appeared on the program to outline the courses in home economics as given at the University of Illinois. In 1903 she made a report for the standing committee on courses of study in colleges and universities saying in part:

"From the first, the conference has recognized the importance of a clearer understanding of the relation of the higher education of the country to those sociological principles which underlie the daily life of the people.

"The first work of this committee was to gather information as to the status of such branches as hygiene, sanitation, economics, etc., in the colleges and universities. A canvass of the country showed that the importance of these branches was *not* generally recognized, that in the agricultural colleges the work was largely on a utilitarian basis without sufficient scientific foundation, that there was danger in allowing this to continue because it would be harder to lift the technical part to a higher plane, the more extended it became. The committee therefore attempted to show in what directions the colleges and universities could bestir themselves, without too definite commitment to a set course of study, to influence opinion along desirable lines."

The statements of the Bevier committee were supplemented by a resolution passed in September, 1902, by the Lake Placid Conference, in which heads of higher institutions were earnestly requested to "consider the advisability of introducing" work in home economics.

At this same meeting Isabel presented a paper on "Physiological Chemistry Taught in Connection with Home Economics."

At the 1904 meeting Isabel again reported on the department at the University of Illinois. Some of the points she made were:

"The organization of the department is somewhat peculiar. For administrative purposes it is allied with the College of Agriculture, and some of its work is offered to students in that college, but as there are no women, the greater proportion of the students come from the College of Literature and Arts.

"In the arrangement of courses of study, as the department aims to give women a liberal education with a basis of pure and applied science, a four-year course planned with that object in view is put in the College of Science.

The entire work of the department is elective, as are other University courses.

"In order to obtain a degree in household science from either the College of Agriculture or from the College of Science, certain prescribed work must be done. The College of Literature and Arts makes the household science work one of its majors. So students may graduate from any one of the colleges, having specialized in household science.

"The strength of the department lies in the fact that it has the advantage of the resources afforded by the various departments of the University. Art, architecture, pure science, literature, history, education, and economic courses are open to its students.

"The department reserves for itself those subjects which especially serve the interest of women, and stand in university life for a recognition of the importance of adequate and proper training for home duties.

"One cannot draw conclusion from a single illustration but judging from results in the University of Illinois there is room for such a department in university life."

The report of the standing committee on Home Economics in Higher Education was given by Caroline Hunt of the University of Wisconsin. In it this sentence appears: "To show that the subject can be presented in an academic manner, we cite the courses given in the University of Illinois and in the University of Chicago." These are the only two universities cited in the entire report. Their inclusion indicates the high reputation of these departments.

By 1905 Isabel was serving as vice-chairman of the conference and chairman of a section on college and university education. Her report summarizing progress at the University of Illinois reflects her interpretation of home economics and indirectly accounts for the success of her work. She saw clearly what she wanted the department to do and was able to steer her course without becoming entangled in the various side issues that plagued many departments.

Isabel reported: "The department is now in its fifth year. Its enrollment for the present year is one hundred and sixty. It stands in university life for those subjects which particularly serve the interests of women. There are twelve courses: three on food emphasizing selection and preparation, economic and dietetic values respectively; three have to do with the house, its sanitation, including house planning, decoration, management; one on chemistry of food and nutrition; one on textiles; one on history and development of home economics as an educational factor; one on public health; and two for graduate work.

"Of the one hundred and thirty credits required for graduation, twenty-five may be obtained in this department. All the work is elective, but in order to obtain a degree in household science certain courses are prescribed.

"Courses are planned for two classes of students: 1) those who specialize in other lines of work but desire a knowledge of the general principles and facts of household science; 2) those who wish to make a specialty of household science by a comprehensive study of the affairs of the home together with the arts and sciences whose applications are directly connected with the management and care of the home. For this latter class two years of work in science, together with courses in art and design, economics, and education are prescribed.

"New courses undertaken in the past year have been: 1) a special course in economics for household service;

2) a course on public health; 3) a summer session course in the interests of rural school teachers.

"The request for a teachers' course is so urgent that one will be offered in this department in connection with the school of education now being organized in the university. Many things yet remain to be done, but there seems to be good reason to believe that in the near future in the University of Illinois household science will be interpreted to mean not merely applied chemistry and physics and bacteriology but also applied economics, ethics, and esthetics."

In 1908 Isabel was first vice-chairman, and a member of three committees: college entrance requirements, national organization, and recommendations.

In a paper, "Outlook for Advanced Work," presented to the Association she stated that advanced work in home economics should emphasize three things:

"1. The orderly development of the subject. There is no sequence in a course which teaches the cooking of potatoes, then the making of chocolate, then creamed cabbage. Lessons should take up food as carbohydrates, fats, etc.

"2. Dietetics. With some this means catering to fads, with others it implies invalid cookery, but in college work it now applies to daily living and means the best results of the combined knowledge and skill of the chemist, the physiologist, and the cook. An institution is judged by its course in dietetics and the requirements for it.

"3. The education value of every subject. There is a noticeable growth of an intelligent public sentiment. People know that home economics means more than food and sewing. They are recognizing its general educational value. At the recent meeting of the National Education Association all sections were discussing industrial training or home economics. As in any new subject, there is a varied nomenclature but this is of little importance."

Of the question of training teachers, Isabel said:

"It is to be remembered that the science of home economics is applied science. It is very necessary for the teacher [of home economics] to know pure science and pure economics. It requires a different kind of teaching to be able to make good applications of pure science, and it would seem to me that it would take more skill to make clear the facts and applications of science to children than to those with more training. From that standpoint our elementary teachers ought to be the best trained in science because they are to make these applications for those who will not have the knowledge to make the corrections as some college students might.

"We do all we can to have our college students remain four years and advise a fifth year if they expect to be college teachers. We recommend no one as a teacher of domestic science who has not taken our course in dietetics. For that we require both chemistry and physiology and the man who gives the work in physiology requires zoology.

"So long as there are places where teachers are made in from six weeks to a year it seems unnecessary to add to that list. We feel that in the present state of development of home economics, with constant criticism of the kind of teachers available, that this conference ought to stand for more rather than less preparation."

When the conference became the American Home Economics Association Isabel continued to be active, serving first as vice-president and later (1911-1913) as its second president. For three years, 1909 to 1912, she was a member of the editorial board of the *Journal of Home Economics,* the official publication of the American Home Economics Association. She represented the division of the House.

Beginning in 1904, Isabel prepared a correspondence course on the house for the American School of Home Economics. The material she used became her book, *The House*.

When the Home Economics Section of the Association of Land Grant Colleges and Universities was formed in 1917, she was made its chairman for two years. She had already appeared on the program of the annual meeting of the Association.

In connection with her activities in state and national organizations and in her role as an educator at the University of Illinois, Isabel spoke to audiences all over the country. She presented papers at the fiftieth anniversary celebrations of both Ohio State University and Purdue University, at Ohio on "The Land Grant College and the Education of Women" and at Purdue on "Contributions of the Land Grant College to Home Economics." In 1923 she addressed the annual meeting of the American Country Life Association on the topics, "Ideals in Home and Family Life in Rural Homes."

Isabel managed, in spite of her many responsibilities, to find time to write. In 1907, with Anna Van Meter, she prepared a laboratory guide, *Selection and Preparation of Food. Science* (February 14, 1908) carried her article, "Problems of Bio Chemistry." In 1913 and 1914 her bulletins, "*Some Points in Making and Judging Bread* and *Planning Meals* were published by the University.

During the years 1914 to 1915 she wrote a series of articles for the magazine, *Woman's World*. These articles dealt with the kitchen, planning meals, buying of food, making bread, and food values. In the June, 1915, issue the editor comments: "With this splendid article on vegetables, their food value, methods of cooking, etc., the head of the Domestic Science Department of the University of Illinois brings her present series to a close. It has made a notable contribution to a subject of vital interest to all women, and the editor of *Woman's World* is glad to have had the privilege of presenting it to his readers."

Isabel Bevier was granted honorary doctorate degrees (D.Sc.) by Iowa State College in 1920 and by Wooster University in 1936. Her name appeared in *"Who's Who in America* and in *American Men of Science.* The American Association for the Advancement of Science showed its appreciation by making her a fellow of that organization. In the councils of educators she was at one time vice-president of one section of the National Education Association, at another, chairman of the home economics section of the Land Grant College Association.* Among national Greek letter societies she was a charter member of the University of Illinois chapter of Sigma Xi, scientific fraternity, honorary member of Sigma Delta Epsilon fraternity of women in science, elected to honorary membership in Phi Beta Kappa by the Wooster chapter, a national honorary member of Phi Upsilon Omicron, and a local honorary member of Omicron Nu, these last two being home economics fraternities.

---

*She was a member of the sub-committee on Nutrition of the National Research Council.

Chapter IV

The Later Years

In 1921 Isabel Bevier resigned from the University of Illinois and set out on the various exploits that were to engage her energies during most of the twenty-one years of her so-called retirement. Freed from departmental responsibility and from the many demands that had accumulated year by year, she could now make new and varied contributions to her chosen field. She would have some quiet time for writing, she thought, but when word of her retirement spread, calls for her services elsewhere altered this plan.

Unable because of her interest in people and in the events around her to refuse the local demands that would come if she remained in Urbana, and unwilling to have her presence embarrass her successor, Isabel decided to seek elsewhere the rest she needed. Characteristically, she put her office and her home in order and was on her way.

She had been asked to go to the University of California at Los Angeles, then known as the Southern Branch. As chairman of the home economics department from 1921 to 1923, she reorganized the work in home economics and taught in the summer session. As always, students came enthusiastically to her classes.

"No one ever joined the faculty who was more eagerly expected and no one on the faculty was ever more helpful," said Dr. Ernest Carroll Moore, Director of the University, some year later. "The University was young and suffering badly from a feeling of inferiority. Miss Bevier brought a stabilizing helpfulness that gave hope and confidence to the entire staff."

Members of the faculty tried to persuade her to continue her work with them. When she said that was impossible, they urged her to "pitch her tent" beside theirs and spend the rest of her days in California. But this also she felt she could not do, and they watched her go feeling that they were losing one who was almost indispensable.

During her stay in California and later Miss Bevier found time to revise her book, *The Home Economics Movement*. Much enlarged and renamed *Home Economics in Education*, it was brought out by Lippincott in 1924. The book was badly needed. Until it was published, anyone wanting to know the details of the home economics movement had to garner the information from a wide variety of sources, some of them difficult to find.

At this time Isabel's two older, unmarried sisters living in Plymouth, Ohio, were seriously ill. In the next few years she was often with them for long periods. Nevertheless, she continued her writing and lecturing, traveling back and forth from east to west, attending conferences, but always carrying her concern for her sisters.

Arizona

Once again, in 1925, she was called into consultation

regarding the reorganization of a department — this time at the University of Arizona. Dr. Cloyd Marvin, who had worked with Isabel when they were both members of the faculty in California, was its new president. During her stay in Tucson she not only helped reorganize the home economics department, but for several months took the place of the head, who was ill, served as a special lecturer, and acted as counselor for vocational guidance, holding conferences with students and giving lectures on vocations open to women. As if this were not enough, she was prevailed upon to make trips for the extension service. One was to Flagstaff by bus, to most people a long, tiresome ordeal, but to Isabel, an experience that held enjoyment "in every mile and every hour."

In Arizona, as in other places, students and faculty warmed to her direct and friendly approaches, the superiority of her intellect, the simplicity and soundness of her judgments. Among the townspeople too, she made friends. She, in turn, loved the desert, the sunsets, the flowers. She made field trips with the archeology group. She visited the observatory on many nights and took a review course in astronomy. The stars were brighter in Arizona, she said, than in any other place she had ever been and this was an opportunity not to be missed. Later, in telling of her experiences in that rough, unfinished country, she summed up her impressions with wry humor: "There is one thing I am sure of, and that is that the end of the world is a long time off. The Lord has too much to do in Arizona yet."

The trips back and forth from California and Arizona to Ohio refreshed her and gave her pleasure. She was fond of travel and, in the words of a friend, she "always traveled to a purpose."

When the needs of her sisters grew more pressing, she gave her full time to bringing what comfort she could to them. She suffered with them, and when in 1927 both sisters died, she felt a need for rest and an entire change of environment. So in the late spring of 1927, with an old schoolmate and life-long friend, she made her third trip to Europe.

Isabel and the Passport Man

While getting ready for this trip, she was asked to go to Washington to represent her Wooster class at a meeting of the American Association of University Women. She persuaded her brother to go with her and, knowing it would be easier to get her passport in Washington than at home, she took him on this errand of which she gives the following characteristic account:

"It was about twelve o'clock, and I suppose the man was hungry and wanted his lunch. In reply to my request for a passport, he said that I could probably get it at home.

" 'No, I can't,' I said. 'I'm here and I want to get it now.'

"He replied, 'You have to have a birth certificate.'

" 'You know as well as I do that birth certificates did not exist when I was born.'

"Then he said that I would have to have proof that I was born. I thought, 'That's easy,' so I said, 'Jack, just come over here and swear that I was born.' Jack replied, 'Well, I can swear. I was there and I know it happened.' "

Apparently this was enough to clear the Bevier passport!

Friends who knew of her plans for this trip abroad, so soon after her sorrowful sojourn with her family in Ohio, sent out word of the date of her sailing. Letters, telegrams, flowers, and other gifts came in a deluge. The purser was so impressed that he referred to her as "the lady with many letters."

Before Isabel left Washington she was asked by Louise Stanley, chief of the U. S. Bureau of Home Economics, to take with her a paper, prepared by Miss Stanley, to read before the International Congress of Agriculture at Rome. For the first time the Congress was to have a section for women. The request led to perhaps the most interesting, if not the most unusual, experience of the trip, an audience with the King of Italy. "Though proud to live in a democracy," Isabel commented, "one may still be curious about the habits of kings."

That she entered into the adventures of this trip with her usual zest is evidenced by her account of the stop at Madeira, where neither the heights nor the toboggan slide daunted her. Bumping downhill over cobblestones in a "kind of willow basket on runners," with two men trotting alongside, proved an alarming adventure to one of her companions but not to her.

Rested after her European trip, she came back in vigorous health, her mind full of stories to tell her friends. She had by no means exhausted her enthusiasm for travel, but she was possibly a little homesick. The fall of 1927 found her again established in Urbana.

For some months it had been clear that she wanted to come home. We were both attending a meeting at Merrill-Palmer School in Detroit early in 1927 when she asked me to go for a walk, which I knew to be a talk since she was careful to exclude any other partners. We hadn't gone far when, taking my arm as she often did when it was to be a confidence (though her confidences were usually given in a stage whisper or a very audible, resonant voice), she began,

"Do you think I've stayed away long enough?" Somewhat bewildered at first, I soon grasped what she had on her mind, for I had suspected all along her real reason for staying away from Urbana. "I thought that if I stayed away about six years it would be long enough so I wouldn't interfere with Ruth [Ruth Wardall, who succeeded her as department head], and I really want to go home." Neither Ruth nor the department, I assured her, would suffer if she returned. Word came before long that she had carried out her wish.

In the years since she retired, Isabel had made only occasional short visits in Urbana. Her house was one she had purchased a few years after going there. On Lincoln avenue near Oregon street, it was unpretentious but pleasant, within comfortable walking distance of the campus and on what was at first a street-car line and afterward a bus line. One room was kept for guests, and after her retirement many and varied were the friends who occupied it. If they chanced to find her early breakfast hour not too comfortable, she made clear that it would be entirely agreeable to her if they wished to sleep late and go to the nearby drugstore for breakfast!

Taking up again the threads of life among her many friends and former colleagues, she was not allowed to remain long inactive. In February, 1928, she was asked by Dean H. W. Mumford, of the College of Agriculture, to become a member of the home economics extension staff to make a survey of the extension work, especially the training of future extension workers. A series of special conferences was also being conducted at this time by the College staff, "which wanted a headline speaker who alone could guarantee the success of the meetings." She was asked to take part.

"A bulwark of strength during worried days," was the way one of her co-workers described her. Her full life and her many contacts had broadened and strengthened her; her clear mind, free from the details of administration, could concentrate on the problems at hand; and she was free to enjoy to the full the beauties of the countryside and her conversations with the extension men and women.

Comparing Old and New

Part of her report to Dean H. W. Mumford at the close of her study describes the changes that had taken place in extension work since she came to Illinois in 1900:

"In the women's session of the Farmers' Institute twenty years ago, the majority of the women were over fifty years old, a rather phlegmatic group somewhat wearied with the struggle, relieved that they were as far along as they were and not keen to undertake new burdens — rather more in the mental state of the woman who announced that 'mostly I'd druther do as I'd druther.' Generally, the officers were women of poise, experience, and ability, but the lay member who read her paper often did it with trembling voice and shaking hands.

"Now the average age I would guess is under forty — women who are in the midst of the battle. They are well-groomed, their stockings are silk, their skirts and hair are short, and their heels are too high for comfort. Their minds are eager, alert, hungry for information on child care and training, on house furnishing, on dyeing, on kitchen equipment, and on numberless other points. They express themselves easily and, for the most part, well. They have definite opinions on many subjects and are interested in self-development."

As in other days, Isabel was fearless and very frank in her remarks, sometimes antagonizing those to whom she was talking by showing them their shortcomings and by reminding them that the broad problems of home economics were more important than petty details. She emphasized the fact that there was real work to be done, not only by the paid workers but by the homemakers themselves, in studying their problems and making plans for the betterment of conditions. Although they had done well, she told them they should not sit back in pride but go on and do more. She did not overlook the men and their responsibility for the success and happiness of the farm home.

"I have done what I could with the time, sense, and strength at my disposal," she said in closing her report. "It seems to me that the future of the work is full of promise and that now is the time to gather the forces and strike often and hard."

Of her contribution to the agricultural adjustment conferences, Dean Mumford wrote:

"Realizing that timely adjustments to ever-changing conditions are essential for the continued progress of Illinois agriculture, the College inaugurated a series of Agricultural Adjustment conferences to be held in various parts of the state. With characteristic and apparently indefatigable energy, Professor Isabel Bevier was one of the principal speakers at the eight regional meetings in 1928 and again in 1929. Her addresses, brilliant with a touch of humor, carried a challenge to both the farmer and the farmer's wife to improve their home life, not only for their own comfort, health, and happiness, but that their children might receive the advantages resulting from the improved home conditions. These improvements pertained not only to home conveniences, but also to the social, cultural and religious advancement of the family.

"These audiences were fortunate to have as a speaker a woman with the background and experience possessed by Professor Bevier, and particularly with her human interest, familiarity with farm conditions, and ambition for their improvement. Her discussion should have gone a long way toward convincing the audiences that the College is as earnest and sincere in its efforts to be of help to the farm home as it is in the solution and adjustment of purely economic problems."

An old friend and associate summed up her contribution to home economics in this way:

"Miss Bevier was not only a pioneer in the home economics movement, but she has gone on consistently keeping the 'home' in home economics both by her teaching and by her practice. This of itself would not be so worthy of note were it not for the fact that the pressure of new forces, and new opportunities as well, is resulting in not a little confusion in camp, as well as some questioning as to just 'where we go from here.' While there is no doubt that Miss Bevier sees justification for some of the new lines of work which are leading home economics far afield, she seems to agree in general . . . that 'there are yet to be found in this country of ours women who make a point of going home in time to get supper.' It is to such women and such homes that Miss Bevier would give a large share of her attention."

In 1929, on Dr. Kinley's retirement from the presidency of the University, Isabel insisted that the time had come for her to retire too. At this second retirement the University showed officially its appreciation of her work by confering on her the title of *professor emerita*, in 1929, the first woman whom the University so honored. "Professor Bevier is one of the members of our faculty to whom we should do all the honor we can," said President Kinley on this occasion. "She built up a great department in the University. She is undoubtedly the foremost woman in her field in the country. She left behind her a great department and sent out into the service of her country a large number of young women who have done fine work in elevating life in the field of their education."

Thus did Isabel sever her last active professional connection with the University of Illinois, though by no means had she retired from active interest in the field of home economics and the affairs of the University.

Europe, 1931

After two years of quiet life in Urbana, Isabel, in 1931, was asked to go on a trip around the world. Although still ready to travel, she felt this too strenuous an undertaking. "I can't see," she said, "any use in going to countries where you have to carry your own bathtub and where they don't really want you anyway. I think I'm a little old to start on that kind of trip." But later in the year when a lively family of four asked her to join them for some months of travel in Europe, she accepted.

Of Isabel's place in the family's activities, the wife wrote: "She made certain terms as to the freedom of her own movements and then decided to go. So began some months of travel, during which Miss Bevier was like a comet in relation to our family's solar system. She owned some attraction to its central group, but was never content to circle around its focus, and darted freely off to yield allegiance to the pull of other foci of her orbit."

She first embarked on a Mediterranean cruise. "I had always dreamed of going to Athens," she said, "but never really expected to. While I was there it snowed and the Acropolis was glorious." At Naples, with its view of Mount Vesuvius, it rained and the rain froze, leaving the mountain gleaming and glistening. When the steam and lava burst forth, the effect was extraordinary."

After landing and going through customs in Naples, she took a taxi to her pension. "I had been told," she said, "that these men were kind of brigands, but I liked the faces of my oarsmen and porter — even though my driver did look like a brigand. After I had been going about fifteen minutes, a blue-coated individual stopped us and talked to the driver. Then the driver said he had to have a dollar and a quarter right away for me and my bags. Usually when I'm not sure of the money, I just get it out and let the driver take it, and I was just ready to do that when I thought to myself, 'You goose, you haven't gone anywhere yet. Maybe you will be stopped several times before you get there.'

"I thought the whole proceeding was queer. Never having been in a holdup, I did not know exactly how to act. I looked at the dial, and it looked to me — if I could read it right — to be something like fifteen cents. Also, they had given me a folder, and that was about what it said, so I said to the driver, 'I don't believe that is true. Anyway, you haven't taken me anywhere. You just take me to the pension and you will be paid.'

"The blue-coated individual and the driver looked at each other and shrugged their shoulders, and then we went on. I felt a little weak after it was all over. When I arrived at the pension, I rushed from the cab and stood not on the order of my going. I said to the porter, 'You pay that man and I'll pay you.' The porter read the dial and then fell on the driver with words I could not understand, and I guess it was just as well that I couldn't. Finally he paid him thirty-five cents."

From Naples Isabel traveled through Italy into Germany, living some weeks in the home of a physician at Heidelberg to acquire more fluency in speaking German. She went to Prague for the International Congress of Agriculture, a session of which she had attended four years before in Rome. One subject they discussed, much to her interest, was "how to keep girls on the farm"; and some English women told of the Woman's Institute in England, which does work similar to extension service in this country. Here she met President Masaryk of Czechoslovakia.

After the Congress came a six-day motor trip through rural Czechoslovakia, with visits to homes and schools. "A much-talked-of kindergarten," she wrote, "proved to be a small garden, a nursery for little plants. The women employed in the garden were given thirty-five cents a day, and the weeds they pulled they took home to feed their geese."

At Interlaken there was *William Tell* played in its natural setting by the townspeople, at Geneva a session of the Opium Conference and sessions of the International Committee of Women of the League of Nations, in London the almshouses, at Stratford Shakespeare being played. A visit to Edinburgh, then back to London, and she was ready to sail for home.

Home Again and Fancy-Free

After this journey Isabel contented herself with travel in the United States, but only once went as far as the Northwest and California. Although the time came when she was willing to be helped onto the train, still, in answer to a call from a sick friend or from one of her alumnae in need of counsel, she was ready to go almost any distance and on very short notice.

Isabel always enjoyed looking in on her "girls." Wherever I was after her retirement she paid me a short visit, the length being of her own choosing. The exact time of arrival and departure was announced in advance.

Her first visit with me was in Washington, D. C., where she had come to do some judging for a magazine. She declined my invitation to stay with me, saying it would be too crowded and too much work for me. I knew better than to insist, but the first night she came to the apartment after our dinner together and glacing around announced without any preliminaries, "We wouldn't be too crowded. I'll have my baggage sent over tomorrow." She did and we had a thoroughly good time.

Her next visit was in Madison, Wisconsin, where she had a good many friends. She arrived with a well thought-out schedule of how she would manage to see them. One friend had just broken her arm. "I'd planned to see her once, but now that she's laid up, I'll go twice," was her decision.

There was a tea in her honor to which not all the home economics faculty had been invited and which was therefore not entirely to her liking. She insisted on leaving the tea almost on the dot. Before we were well off the porch she took my arm and in her stage whisper, with a touch of mischief, said, "Now we can take that drive around the lake," and I recalled having told her that if we were through in time, we would take the road around Lake Mendota, a drive she always enjoyed. She seemed never to tire of automobile riding, usually bringing out of her purse a roll or two of hard candies before we had gone our first mile. Unlike some of my younger friends, she liked to ride with the top of the convertible down, and once at her own request she took a turn in the rumble seat — a stylish "trunk" seat of those days.

Next came Swarthmore, Pennsylvania, and a longer visit this time, since I had a good housekeeper to take care of our needs. Relishing our long drives through the rolling country, Isabel was reluctant to give time to social affairs. Yet there were several friends she was eager to see, and a great many people who wanted to see her. To the suggestion that we have a tea, she responded with an unqualified, "No." The next morning, however, she called me into her room. She was sitting on the side of her bed, one shoe on and one in her hand. "I've been thinking about that tea and I've changed my mind. I don't want to take time to see all of those people individually. If I do I'll not have time for anything else. Let's go ahead and have the tea and I can see them all in one day."

Next came Washington again in 1934. My apartment was in a walk-up in a made-over house on H Street, just off 17th. I rather discouraged her staying with me, but she was not daunted by the three flights of stairs nor by the fact that I would have to be out of town for a few days. Withstanding the urging of friends who might have made her more comfortable, she stayed on in my apartment. It was, she said, "in the midst of things." I suspected too that she liked the independence I gave her. While I was away, her friends could call, and I made few suggestions as to how she should spend her time.

Isabel attended ceremonies honoring Jane Addams, whom

she knew and greatly admired. Together we did our usual driving about and went to at least one movie. Each day while I was at work, she was out on a lark of her own. One evening, however, I was surprised to find she had been in the apartment all day. She was noncommital and I did not press my inquiry. It was a day to catch up, she said. But before she left she confessed that her knees had seemed about to give way and she had said to herself, "You'd better take care of yourself or you'll be sick on Lita's hands, and she must not have that, busy as she is."

When I returned to the University of Illinois in 1936, after thirteen years' absence, I found Isabel Bevier living comfortably in the house that had been her home for so many years. A grandniece, Mary Morrow, was "taking care of me," as Isabel expressed it; but Mary, I am sure, felt she had her share of being looked after.

Still very active, Isabel was reviewing her French via radio, studying suitable texts and carefully writing out assignments. She displayed a map she had drawn as part of her Bible study, explaining, "It's supposed to be a map of Paul's journeys, but I'm not very good at drawing." The pink jacket she was knitting was for the expected baby of a former member of the faculty. The various calls she had been making the past few days were in the interest of a project of the League of Women Voters.

When the day came for the first University Senate meeting after my return, she suggested that I meet her there. "I always sit in the middle up front," she said. "It's a little conspicuous when there are so few women, but it's the only way I can be sure of hearing." The Senate, I might explain, is composed of all the full professors of the University. "Emeritus professors may attend," she commented with mock solemnity, "but I don't think they're supposed to say anything unless they're called on."

While not particularly clothes-conscious in day-to-day work, she liked to wear dressy clothes for festive occasions. After retirement she sometimes attended professional meetings, chiefly, by her own confession, to visit with the people in attendance. When the crowd was gathering for one banquet I knew she had no intention of attending, she appeared in her best lace dress. She circulated from one group to another, chatting gaily. As she passed me, she paused to whisper that when they started to go into the banquet hall she was going to her room and to bed. This is exactly what she did after courteously evading several offers to escort her to one of the tables.

These episodes, small in themselves, are told in an effort to piece together a complex personality — to give some suggestion of the very human side of this unusual woman.

Eightieth Birthday Celebration

Although Isabel never lost interest in her friends, family, and profession, and was for the most part in good health as she approached her eighties, her vigor began to lessen and she suffered some impairment of hearing. At last, when she thought she was "missing too much," she resorted to a hearing aid for occasional use. When the salesman was telling her of ways to conceal the battery, she finally interrupted with, "I see no reason to conceal it." Nor did she try to conceal the one she finally chose. She wanted an effective aid, and that was all.

As her eightieth birthday approached, the home economics faculty began planning to celebrate it. I was delegated to find out what would be most pleasing to her. Armed with taffy apples, I took her to one of our favorite spots for watching the sunset, and when darkness was almost upon us, I broached the subject.

She wanted no celebration. The faculty had done too much for her as it was. She was getting deaf and wasn't very good at social things. There was more, and from long experience I knew there was nothing to do but listen until she had talked herself out in monologue fashion.

When my turn came to speak, I assured her that she would have to leave town if she were to avoid a celebration of some sort. That gave her pause, and I was able to tell her what had been discussed — a dinner or afternoon reception at the University Women's Club. If it had to be — and I could see that she was becoming interested — it had better not be a dinner, for you had no chance to talk to anybody except those near you, and a reception at the club was a touch-and-go affair.

Then I proposed a tea at my house. This struck the right chord. Guests wouldn't come in crowds and there would be no time limit. I was to promise not to insist upon "all the young assistants who hardly know me" attending as a duty.

As a matter of fact, almost every one of the faculty and former members of the faculty came, and I know of no one who felt it a duty call. Isabel was in high spirits — she had on a new blue dress, sat in her favorite chair when she wanted to rest, and made of it a gala performance for all of us. It was well after seven o'clock before the last guest left.

Nearing the End

After the holidays two years later, in 1942, while showing

96

me her tree and the gifts around it, she said that that Christmas had been one of the best she had ever had. She recounted the social things she had done — enough to weary a much younger woman. But when going home from a party early in January, she seemed unusually quiet, and I asked her if she felt well. She said she did but was tired. On Twelfth Night she sent word that she was going to the University hospital but didn't expect to be there long and didn't want people to know. She had had a heart attack and Dr. Draper, son of the president who brought her to the University, thought the hospital was the best place for her.

She stayed in the hospital until early March, then went home. She was better for a while, then not so well. On my office calendar of March 15, I find this jotting, placed there after my daily visit: "a courageous, intelligent woman meeting the inevitable." Two days later, on March 17, she died. She was buried in the Bevier family plot in Plymouth, Ohio.

When her will was read it was found to contain a paragraph giving to the Board of Trustees of the University of Illinois the sum of five thousand dollars, the income from which was to be used by the Board as a lecture fund for the Department of Home Economics. The general theme of the lectures, which she specified, was to be "the philosophy of home economics, or, stated in another way, [they] are to deal with the scientific, economic, esthetic, and social aspects of home and family life, in order that the woman so trained may be enabled to apply this knowledge in her daily tasks in her home, family, and community life in accordance with the finest intellectual and spiritual ideals."

That was the only item in her will she had ever mentioned to me, and she charged me to see to it that "the brethren," as she called them, used the money for home economics and not for some other cause they might think more worthy on this campus where men's interests, she believed, usually had first consideration.

The Bevier Lectures

Dr. Henry C. Sherman, Mitchill Professor of Chemistry at Columbia University, gave the first lecture, "Food and Nutrition Today and Tomorrow," on May 15, 1945.

"No words can express my gratification," Dr. Sherman began, "in the honor of this call to speak on your campus in appreciation of our mutual friend, Isabel Bevier, whom I met as a fellow chemist forty-seven years ago when we were both assisting in Professor Atwater's nutrition investigations, and whom I have ever since held in the very highest esteem.

"After the topic for this lecture had been settled, I learned that the series of annual lectures of which this is the first are expected, as the years roll 'round, to cover many aspects of life, yet to be unified through the fact that all are to bear upon 'the philosophy of home economics.' And Professor Bevier seems to have put 'philosophy' in quotes to mark it as admitting of individual interpretation.

"Today's talk will deal with the most practical of our concerns, our daily food; yet, like most scientific lectures, it aims to be philosophical in the literal sense of appealing to the love of learning.

"We want to know, as exactly as we can, the nature of today's view of food and nutrition, and of the new power that comes with our new knowledge and insight in this field."

After his usual scholarly and delightful presentation of

his subject, he closed with this forward look: "Ending as we began, with an invocation of the spirit of the Bevier Lectureship, may we each carry with us throughout a to-morrow long enough to bring it into effect, this thought: that the *How* of excellent nutrition for all is not too difficult a problem for this generation when we also remember its *Why* — that this is a good goal in itself, and that, more importantly than any previous generation could conceive, we now see that it implements all other human endeavors."

The opening and closing paragraphs of the second Bevier lecture, *The Heritage of Home Economics in Illinois*, by Frances L. Swain, retired director of home economics in the Chicago public schools, and a life-long friend of Miss Bevier are included here because they show how Isabel's personality, her homely advice, and her wisdom stayed as an intimate part of the thought and experience of the younger professional women who came into close associa-tion with her.

"I am deeply honored," Miss Swain said, "to be invited to come to this University in response to the mandate of Miss Isabel Bevier's will. It would be presumptuous for me to attempt to add honor to her name, but I do have a vivid picture of the way she urged us to 'stand up and speak up to the best of your ability.' I should be untrue to her exam-ple and her teaching if I did not do my best in handing on what I have of inspiration and information concerning the earlier leaders in home economics in our state of Illinois."

Frances Swain spoke of the fortunate contacts Illinois had enjoyed with Ellen Richards and continued: "By no means the least influential of Mrs. Richards' students to come to Illinois was Isabel Bevier, whose name has been given permanence in this University where she worked so long and so well for home economics. . . . I should like to leave with you a definition of home economics which Miss Bevier gave to me one day: 'The purpose of home economics is to interpret through the daily task and in the common life ideals and standards for individual, home, and community life.'"

After telling briefly of prominent Illinois home economists, Miss Swain closed her talk with: "In *Plutarch's Lives* we find a paragraph which describes the value of a background of knowledge of the past: 'It was for the sake of others that I first commenced writing biographies; but I find myself proceeding and attaching myself to it for my own; the virtues of these great men serving me as a sort of looking glass in which I may see how to adjust and adorn my own life. Indeed it can be compared to nothing but daily living and associating together; we receive, as it were, in our inquiry . . . and select from their actions all that is noblest and worthiest to know . . . what more effective means to one's moral improvement.' It is with a recognition of this value of biography as well as a desire to pay tribute to the women who laid the foundations on which you are building that I ask you to remember with gratitude our heritage in Illinois."

The next lectures were given in 1950 under the general title, "What Education for Women?" Dr. Florence Kluckhohn, Lecturer and Research Associate in the Department of Social Relations at Harvard University, spoke on the topic, "Women — America." Dr. Bancroft Beatley, President of Simmons College, took for his subject, "Another Look at Women's Education." In introducing the speakers, Dr. Janice M. Smith, head of the Home Economics Department at the University of Illinois, paid tribute to Isabel Bevier:

"The education of women in college was a subject on which Miss Bevier had written with great insight. In 1918 she wrote 'Home Economics has a chance to teach something of the beauty of life and the unity of life, to teach that there is an art in a well-ordered home and a well-ordered life; and that perhaps is the greatest thing that home economics has to do.'

"And in 1925, 'Women need . . . to remember it is their God-given business to mother the race. For this high and holy calling no courage is too great, no sacrifice too costly, no education too high.'

"Surely few faculty women in the annals of the University of Illinois or in the whole breadth of Home Economics have left such a memory — of understanding, vision and inspiration.

"Strength, courage, wisdom, a keen sense of humor, high intelligence and purpose are some of the qualities mentioned by those who knew her. Those of us in Home Economics are particularly grateful for the wisdom she evidenced in the early plans for the work here."

After pointing out in some detail the various roles of women in present-day American society and their problems Dr. Florence Kluckhohn said in part:

"From the educational point of view what we have done and are still doing is to train our young girls for independent autonomous roles which in patterning are extremely similar to masculine roles. But it is education, as has been indicated, largely on a contingency basis. They should expect to act independently only if necessity demands. Typically they are asked to forsake such autonomy upon marriage and assume a representative role — the general domestic one, for which they have very seldom been systematically trained.

"Since the small or nuclear American family is such that members characteristically interact with the outside world as independent agents, the burden put upon the wife and another of having to assume a dependent representative role is considerable. Today with families smaller than ever and with urban patterns having supplanted the neighborhood pattern of other years, the problem of isolation has become acute.

"Thus it is that even though American women have won a relatively high legal, moral and political status, even though they exercise an influence and dominance which is unknown to the women of most societies, they are not generally content or very well adjusted. They are confused and everyone else is confused about them. . . .

"Clearly, what is called for is the kind of thinking and the kind of education which will make of the woman's role a bifurcated one, permitting a combination of a limited occupational activity and a truly creative domestic role. The goal of interesting women in their homes and training them for the work is a goal of first importance, but it must coincide, perhaps even follow, a recognition of women's right to have a defined place in the economic structure for which she is also trained.

"The basic educational problem is that of educating both men and women for the attitudinal acceptance of such an integrated role. Much of this must be achieved at early ages in our homes. Schools and colleges can do much more than they now do to further such attitudinal change. More specific training in schools and colleges for both aspects of the role can also be developed, but again it is idle to suppose that the mere inclusion of courses devoted to the domestic arts will have much of the effect we desire until the attitudes toward the value of domestic activities is vastly altered from what it now is. . . .

"What we can do by way of educating women in our schools and colleges for the specifically feminine domestic role is severely limited by the deeply rooted cultural attitude that education is the same for all, regardless of sex or other differences.

"It is this attitude, in combination with the culturally defined belief that all activities should be made rational and scientific, which has led to a slanting of what domestic training there is in the scientific direction. It is, in other words, no accident that homemaking programs were once called domestic science and that college departments now carry the title 'Home Economics.' Could it be that more stress upon the artistic and less upon the scientific would bring a change in the evaluation of domesticity by both women and men? Has even motherhood, as mothers let themselves be governed by the latest book, become more a science than an art of human relationships?

"These are speculative suggestions within the frame of the more certain argument that efforts, strenuous efforts, must be made to alter prevailing attitudes both toward the domestic aspect of the feminine role and the role of women as productive members of our occupational system. . . .

"We do need to utilize, much better than we now do, the energies of our women in full, do need to give women an opportunity for an expression of their various abilities and the special trainings provided by American education, but we cannot do this at the expense of family life. Let us then train women for jobs that are typically women's jobs in time and scope, and at the same time train them for domestic functions which social rewards and not moral diatribes declare to be both valuable for and indispensable to our whole society. There is no cultural law which states that persons must confine themselves to one kind of activity. It is our one great fault as a people that, loving achievement and success as we do, we have asked all competitors to put their cars on one and the same track — the economic one. Perhaps it will be the great contribution of our women to lay bare the fallacy in such reasoning."

Dr. Bancroft Beatley opened his discussion of women's education with a brief review of its history in our country. In his opinion, "the issue today is not whether women can pursue the same collegiate program as men, but whether they *ought* to do so in view of the different roles that men and women play in our common life. There is a growing body of evidence that women's education needs re-examination." He then cited proof of this need and concluded by saying:

"One of the most obvious improvements needed in women's education today is the offering of instruction in homemaking, at least to the extent of home management and child guidance, in all colleges attended by women, and the encouragement of all women students to include in their programs some experience in this area. In common with civic education, education in homemaking is a 'must' if we accept the logical deductions of the functional theory as applied to the education of women. . . .

"Many uninformed persons think of vocational or technical education as synonymous with training in skills. Though some marketable skill must result from vocational education, the higher the occupational level the more the training must emphasize technical intelligence. Since the occupations which college women will seek to enter are of a professional or at least semiprofessional character there is a large body of facts, ideas, and principles on which successful work in these occupations depends. Technical intelligence is the *what* and the *why*, rather than the *how*. All the skill in the world in the preparation of food will not make a sound nutritionist. She must first of all be a competent student of dietetics. Dietetics, in turn, is an organized body of subject-matter drawing its materials from such established disciplines as chemistry, physiology, pathology, physics, economics, sociology, and psychology. Skills are an essential and worthy part of job preparation, but we must relate them constantly to the fundamental ideas and principles which constitute technical intelligence. If we do this, we can be confident that our graduates will qualify initially for positions in fields that challenge their abilities, and that they will have the basis for progressive growth toward positions of larger responsibility commanding their best efforts."

Considering Isabel Bevier's interest in the house, the lecture given March 16, 1953, by James Marston Fitch, architectural editor of *House Beautiful,* on the subject, "The American House at Mid-Century," seemed particularly fitting. The following few paragraphs taken from his notes will show the general trend of his talk.

He said: "In the house, as in other areas, we stand astride two eras. And we will be better able to plot our course in the new era if we better understand the old.

"If this is so, then it is a happy coincidence which brings us together here in Illinois this evening. For it is precisely here in the Midwest that these forces can be traced with especial clarity. . . .

"The main effect of industrialization has been to change the house, even the farm house, from a center of production to a center of consumption. And the most conspicuous architectural evidence of this has been the shrinking size of the house. . . .

"Yet diminishing size is the least important aspect of what has happened to the houses: its changing function is what matters. I said a while back that a direct causal line connects the first McCormick reapers with the first houses by Frank Lloyd Wright. For Wright's houses were the first expression, at a high architectural level, of the changed society which Mr. McCormick and his kind had wrought. They were the first expression of the modern house in its urbanized, economically nonproductive role. . . .

"A house is a tool, a complex instrument, for manipulating your environment. It is of course different from most other tools if for no other reason than that you live in it. It affects — I might almost say, it controls — more aspects of your life than you dream of — your work and rest, concentration and relaxation, moods and emotions. You experience a house with all your senses: sight, hearing, touch, smell. Temperatures, drafts, odors, noises, glare and gloom, all have a direct bearing on your well-being. Therefore when it comes to a house don't judge it by looks alone.

"Now I do not mean to imply that there's anything wrong with a house being good to look at; in fact, any really good house must by definition satisfy our esthetic as well as our practical requirements. But looks are only one measure of its worth. Here ordinary common sense is a good solvent. Instead of asking yourself: Do I like the looks of this house? ask yourself: Do I like the feel of this house? Do I like its sound? Do I like its smell? In short, what is its all-around performance? . . .

"If the house tradition established by Wright and the

Greene Brothers seems more promising today than these glass cages [he had just discussed houses in which large amounts of glass are used], it is largely because they have recognized two simple facts: the nature of our climate and the nature of man himself. They have recognized that there are times when we want the flooding sunlight of a greenhouse, times when we need the close security of a cave. Times when we need the broad expansive outlook, times when we need privacy. Actually, a good house should provide both. The chief virtue of modern house-building technology is that it can do just that. . . .

"You will have noticed I imagine that I have preached a sermon on the golden mean. There is no cause for undue pessimism, certainly none for uncritical optimism. Our houses stand in much the same state as our society as a whole. And because they reflect so accurately our values and mores as a people they can only deteriorate or improve as we do ourselves."

Isabel Bevier's books, her lectures, and her articles supplement her accounts of her years of preparation and her work at Illinois. In them she expressed her philosophy of home economics. The material which appears here for the first time and the reprinted excerpts are her revelation of what she knew and felt about home economics and the education of women.

Summary of the Bevier Philosophy

Because her lectures and her articles represent her professional self they contain fewer glimpses of her rare personality but reveal more of her rare mind. And most of what she wrote is not "dated." Her chief interest was in educating women to be capable, attractive, influential members of their homes and their communities. She recognized that women have a different role in society from that of men. In a period when "the right to compete" was a feminist battle cry, she looked beyond competition to a supplementing of the work and thought of men. She believed women should be offered more than "a blind imitation of the education of men" — that their educational opportunities should be different because their objectives are different. Since her ideas forecast those of many educators today who are especially interested in the direction which women's education shall take, what Isabel Bevier had to say as an intellectual pioneer is of as lasting interest as her work in home economics.

Her liberal arts and specialized training, her interest in the political, social, and economic responsibilities of women, together with her experience in high school and college work, combined to lend authority to her opinions. She examined the problem of suitable college education for women thoughtfully from many angles and came to her conclusions after years of study, observation, and experience.

Her clear-cut ideas and definiteness of purpose gave significance to all she said in her lectures. In one sense the quotations given in this book let her speak again. In another sense quotations are not quite enough, for it was not entirely what she said but the way she said it that appealed to her audience and gave her words the influence they had.

Isabel's Charm

The records of Isabel's lectures reflect only imperfectly the richness of the talk itself. Stimulating as her words are, they do not convey to the reader the effect of the address on the people who heard her give it — the feeling of elation in any audience where her clear, far-ranging thinking found its way into spoken words.

She spoke with greatest charm when the talk was impromptu and informal. When she "committed it to paper," as she expressed it, she left out many of the asides we had especially enjoyed. We often told her so and she responded with a chuckle and a promise to do better. But even if we had a record of the unexpected humorous comment and the apt illustrations that enlivened her speech under the stimulus of an audience, there would still be missing the warmth of her voice, the animation of her face, and the strong magnetism of her physical vitality.

She could challenge the thinking of an academic group or appeal to the common sense of a popular audience. Comments made by a reporter on a small town newspaper about a talk by Isabel in 1917 give some idea of the impression she made on her audience.

"The best talk of all was made by Miss Bevier, who is head of the Household Science Department. I supposed she would be very scientific and tell us about a lot of things that would be all right for people who had money and lived in town and had all the modern conveniences, but she was very practical and I thought how glad we ought to be to have a woman like her in our state university. Girls who go there to school won't get any foolish impractical ideas from her, you may be sure. One of the best things she said was that men thought women were unbusinesslike and did not know how to take care of money. But she said that it was because they were never told to spend wisely but always told they must save. She said she would like to have the pocketbook transferred to the woman for one week and for that time the man should have full control of the butter-

and-egg money to buy what he needed, and she would choose that time when the hens were moulting and the cows were dry.

"I was glad to have her say that we will always be obliged to wash dishes and cook meals and keep our houses clean. I never have had much faith in those who tell you that you ought to be able to press a button and do the dishes or turn a crank and have the washing done. But it is true we are doing a lot of unnecessary work and things we could get rid of if we only set our minds to it. She told about the woman intending to make a cake who had to climb up on a chair to get the recipe out of the cup on the third pantry shelf. I don't know whether she knew that I keep mine there and that every time I make an angel cake I have to go over all the recipes to find that one.

"The subject of her lecture was 'After the New House-keeping What?' It wasn't to be buying food out of a can or everyone living in a boarding house. It was merely to be better housekeepers, with more time for rest and relaxation and enjoyment and being able to do some of the things we wanted to do. I was glad that so many of the *Review* readers could hear her talk, but I wish that every housewife in Illinois might have heard her."

Chapter V

Ideas Into Action

ISABEL BEVIER came to Illinois with a perceptive, open mind. She quickly made use of her training in developing a curriculum suitable to a land-grant college. Enthusiastic, though never fanatic, she advocated educating women for the life most of them would lead as wives and mothers.

Her interest in science and the home predates Illinois, going back to Dr. Atwater's laboratory and her work with bread, to her study of the nutritive problems of the Negroes, and to her work in sanitary engineering with Mrs. Richards. But except for her course on chemistry and food, developed earlier, her applications were made at Illinois and there her educational theories came to a focus.

She was consistently unwilling to offer college courses devoted almost entirely to skills, unwilling to mortgage the students' time with specialized home economics subjects to the point where courses in history, economics, literature, and art were crowded out. She stood for a liberal college course with a major only in home economics.

Isabel's Book

She did not see home economics as isolated from the long

evolution of ideas regarding formal education, but as a logical development. She believed home economics students must be given this feeling of continuity and some understanding of the difficulties the movement had faced if they were to comprehend fully their opportunities and obligations as home economists. With this in mind she taught a course on the home economics movement and with Susannah Usher in 1906 wrote a small text, as previously mentioned. Revised, it was published in 1924 as *Home Economics in Education*. This book has been valuable to persons charged with the responsibility of interpreting and guiding the destinies of the home economics movement. She dedicated it, "To my girls, who for many years have been my inspiration and my pride." Her "girls" were her students, and the dedication of her most important publication reflects her deep regard for them.

The first sentence of *Home Economics in Education* states its purpose: to consider the development of home economics and its relation to the higher education of women. Isabel comments that "lack of suitable historic background has often been responsible for wrong ideas in regard to modern movements in education." Dating the idea of vocational education back to the sixth century B.C., with skill and discrimination she traces the history of ideas out of which grew the modern conception of home economics.

Isabel Bevier's careful study of the problems involved in the education of women was evident in every phase of her work. Her awareness of the past enabled her to understand the present more completely and fit home economics into the needs of the twentieth century.

As early as 1898, two years before coming to the University of Illinois, Isabel gave an address before the Domestic

Science Department of the Mechanics' Charitable Association of Boston which was reported in *The American Kitchen Magazine* of December of that year under the title, "The U. S. Government and the Housewife." In it she discussed the nutrition investigations then being carried on in the U. S. Department of Agriculture and included some quotations from Bulletin No. 28, *The Chemical Composition of American Food Materials,* an early landmark known to all students of nutrition. Her two closing paragraphs are so revealing of her common-sense attitude that they are quoted here.

May I be allowed to offer a word of protest here against spending time and money in making marvelous combinations for indigestible desserts? A sort of "food fancy work," with far too much *fancy* and too little *food* for human nature's good. Doubtless fancy work has its place in the world, but most people prefer pillows to pillow shams, and a well broiled steak to puff-paste.

I neither expect nor desire any sudden revolution in reference to our daily diet. Probably your brothers and mine will continue to eat pie, and I see no occasion for hysterics on our part if they do; but I do confidently expect that there will come gradually into all our homes, a domestic science more worthy of the name, and that the American housewife will learn to think in terms of nutritive value.

Thus her sanity, patience, and good humor brought a statistical paper to a happy close. The paper itself reflects the combination of qualities she was to bring into the new educational movement when in two years she became head of the household science department at the University of Illinois. As a scientist she insisted her information have statistical proof obtained through research, but her interpretation and her recommendations were always something the homemaker "could live with," as she often remarked.

Although on various occasions Isabel expressed her feeling that art could be brought into all the practical activities of the home, she perhaps never did so more pointedly than in a talk which she called, "Art in the Home."

Possibly this subject suggests to many of you that I am about to speak of rugs from the Orient, paintings by the old masters, marbles from Italy, treasures from many lands.

But for such an undertaking I have neither the requisite knowledge nor the desire. I wish rather to see how the principles of art may be applied in our homes to the daily tasks and the common life. . . .

The table that looks as if a whirlwind had struck it is not artistic.

The products of home activities come under these rules of art. The indiscriminate mess of fruit and vegetables sometimes placed before one as a salad, the spanked biscuit, and the lopsided loaf of bread are sometimes found where art is interpreted to mean abundant leisure and an oil painting. That group of people is often more interested in the *"The Angelus" in art* than in *art in the home*.

I have spoken thus because it seems to me the women's clubs of our country can do much in bringing the art spirit into homes and communities if they will turn their attention to it. Lorado Taft said he felt the *extension-education* women had gone much further in teaching art in common life than the sculptors because they had begun where the rural woman wanted help — in the use of color in her clothing. They had taught her both form and color, largely by showing her how to dress becomingly and furnish her house artistically.

Chapter VI

Special Opinions

Men in Household Science

In a memorandum to the student newspaper, *The Daily Illini*, 1905, Isabel protested the University catalog's implication that "household science" was for women only. She felt the subject was of value to men as well as to women and important in the whole program of public health. In stressing the idea that physicians should know something of the nutritive values of food, she was advancing an idea new to most people in 1905. She labeled her protest, "A Misapprehension."

The last number of the University Bulletin voices an opinion that is quite too prevalent concerning the work of departments of household science. Most people have rather a hazy and indefinite idea concerning the courses offered in such departments, but feel that they can speak definitely with regard to one fact concerning their work; namely, that it belongs to women only. They apparently forget for the moment the statement that is always made concerning such a department, namely, that it has to do with the affairs of the home, that it deals with the essentials of life, air, water, food, shelter, and clothing. If these statements are kept in mind it is easy to see that courses in this department are not based upon sex lines.

As all human beings need air and water, food and shelter, it is quite desirable that all human beings should have some knowledge concerning these essentials, so courses in domestic architecture are of interest and value alike to men and women. It is quite desirable that both should understand the principles of construction, the requirements of good building, the principles of decoration. Again, in these days in the treatment of diseases more importance is laid often upon the food given the patient than upon the medicine. It is therefore most desirable that a working knowledge of the selection, preparation, nutritive, and dietetic value of food should constitute a part of the training of the physician. As a matter of fact, medical students of the Massachusetts General Hospital have been known to take such courses. Again, the individual home can realize its ideals of sanitary and esthetic requirements only in an atmosphere of strong public sentiment in this regard.

There is a strong demand that the question of public health shall be made a part of the training of the youth of the land. One can but feel that if the topics suggested above should be included in the training of college students, both men and women, its results would be seen in better houses, more beautiful surroundings, cleaner streets, and the Board of Health would not so often feel that their entire duty to their municipality had been served when they had provided a pest house, but neglected the question of safe water or the disposal of sewage and garbage.

Bevier the Writer

When she was preparing her writing for publication, Isabel edited it carefully. Her conception of formal writing, part of her liberal arts training, made for dignified and forceful prose. But when she was composing a first draft or when she was speaking extemporaneously, she could not repress her humor or her gay disrespect for all that was stuffy and pretentious, especially in educational theory. Among her papers appears a fragmentary, rough draft, with notes penciled between the typing, of her trenchant comments given in Iowa City in 1909 on, "The Trend Toward the Practical in Education."

The "trend toward the practical in education" is one of a dozen titles under which the disapproval of our present public school system is expressed. Under whatever term discussed, the conclusion seems unfailing that something is the matter with the public schools. I feel assured that you have little interest this morning in tracing the history of the steps by which we have arrived at this condition. As someone says, "It is not necessary for each of us to burn our hands in order to know that fire burns. Our neighbors' scars are often sufficient to convince us." And I am equally certain that I would not have been asked to stand in this place at this time if there had not been in your heart the hope that I might contribute in some small degree to the answer to that other universal question, "What are you going to do about it?" Realizing the limitations of both my experience and knowledge, and feeling assured that no single opinion will be of any great value, such as I have I give gladly, trusting that in intention, at least, I shall not disappoint your hope.

Bevier's Great Defense of the Schools

Let me bring to your mind, if I may, two pictures: the interior of a public school building, and the throng outside.

Inside are the crowded rooms, with all the paraphernalia of the modern classroom — charts, pictures, globes, blackboards, and apparatus of many kinds — as well as an eager, restless throng of pupils and a somewhat tense teacher. The company represents all shades of thought and feeling, but teacher and pupil alike apparently agree in a desire to get through with the thing in hand so as to be ready for the next to which that bell will certainly call. (Pupils *get through* with subjects these days or *get them off*, not *in*.)

Little wonder if at the close of the day both are wearied with the chase rather than enriched mentally and morally by the journey. The teacher says, "Oh dear, I didn't get half through with the things I hoped to do." The conscientious pupil thinks with dismay of the failure to recite. The dullard goes with joy to the game he really likes.

The throng on the outside are loud in their condemnation of what is being done on the inside. Even though many of them are quite ignorant of what is being attempted, they are sure something is wrong, and apparent proof is given to their statement by the numbers who leave the school before the eighth grade is reached and by inefficiency all along the line. Little wonder if the tension on the inside makes abnormal relations seem normal and if in the din, confusion, and misapprehension of the outside, confusion inside be not worse.

Comparing Schools with Industry

Surely this is a time for some thinking, for sympathetic investigation, for careful discrimination between essentials and nonessentials, and for a cheerful optimism that realizes how much worse off we might be, in fact have been. We ought to realize, it seems to me, that some of our difficulties are due to growing pains. We hear much fulsome oratory about the tremendous scale in which everything is being done in the United States. Adjectives fail. *Industry, art, and science each confesses its inability to keep pace* — why should the school system, which is the mirror of this complex life, be expected to keep pace? Why, I have had in my high-school classes boys who grew so much in one night that they could not tell the next morning how far either their voice or their feet would reach if let loose. How could you expect a day school system to care for a nation of them?

For years we trained the brain, or tried to, as if there were no hands in this body which housed the brain. Some enthusiasts now seem likely to go as far to the other extreme and to act as though a skilled hand could be secured without any reference to the brain to direct it or to the body of which it is a part. "Efficiency" is the test word now. Idealism is pronounced very impractical and culture quite unnecessary. True, some so-called culture always has been and always will be quite unnecessary, but the kind which Dr. Draper thus defines will always be useful: "Culture worth seeking in or out of the schools must come from labor upon things worth doing and from the influence of the power to do and the pleasure of real accomplishment upon the soul of the one who does."

In the final analysis the world has always wanted and still wants cultured men and women, capable with brain and hand; with moral backbone enough to do what they believe is right as God gives them the power to see the right, and these men and women have come and will still come from the ranks of the public school.

What then shall be done with the school programs?

The things that are in them only because *they have always been in them* shall be scanned and probably largely eliminated. Illustrations shall be taken from daily life rather than Greece and Rome. Not all forms of the savage state need be illustrated in the work given. Some children pass through several of those stages in a week and some of them better not be illustrated. The briefest allusion to or acquaintance with a cat, a worm, or a fish better not be designated as nature study and classified as concepts or precepts. The child ought to learn to use and appreciate the English language. If he must give himself to the battle of life, to earning bread and butter even after he leaves school, let him have tucked away safely in his memory some words of inspiration for his hour of need.

Shall we have vocational studies? Surely. Shall we have cultural studies? Surely. Inside this schoolroom we are to have the life that now is on the outside of it, so that the exit to the life outside shall not leave the individual stranded and useless, not knowing how to find his place or do any small part of his share of the world's thinking or doing. It must send him out not only good but good for something. Because these children are human beings, universal human needs must be considered in the program. They must know how to meet the primal needs of food, shelter, and clothing, how to live and work with others.

So much for general principles. In these days of psychological pedagogy and pedagogical psychology I read that women do not understand how to deal with boys, so I leave them to men and limit the further remarks that I have to make to what may be expected of girls in the public schools.

The remainder of Isabel's spirited paper on the practical in education has been lost. However, her conviction that a practical education for a girl provides her with an appreciation of her place in life, technical skills in household management, and a good business sense is evident in the paper she presented before the North Central Association of Colleges and Schools meeting in Chicago on March 25, 1911.

"Home Economics in the High School and University" reflects the careful consideration she had been giving to the phases of home economics suited to teaching programs in elementary school, high schools, and colleges. As chairman of the syllabus committee of the American Home Economics Association and the moving spirit behind the syllabus published by the University of Illinois, she wielded a great influence in shaping teaching programs. Comparing her ideas in the following paper with the contents of the two syllabi convinces one of the close relationship between them. Records of her part in discussion at Association meetings furnish further evidence of the strength of her influence.

High School and College Homemaking

As I see it the main purpose of this work in both high school and university is the same, viz., to provide, as an integral part of the girl's training, work with the materials, the processes, and products of the home to the end that the girl may go from both high school and university with some appreciation of the place of woman in home and family life, with a first-hand knowledge of its processes, some technical skill in, and business sense concerning them. The necessity for such work is due, as you all know, very largely to changed conditions, to the pressure of modern life, to the evils of specialization, which provides one teacher to train the head and another the feet of the girl, and yet another to care for her morals. Explain it as you will, the fact remains that the girl in the home even of the middle class knows little of the processes of the home.

I have thus hastily sketched some tangible results to be obtained by work in domestic science in the high school, but I would remind you that the most valuable results are often those which yield themselves least easily to listing processes — or catalog systems. This seems to me particularly true of results of domestic science work. Who shall say what inspiration for better living conditions, what aspirations for purer social and personal ambition are fostered by this work?

When we come to consider the part of home economics in the university, the horizon is widened by the better training of the student, the longer time, the larger liberty of choice in the offerings. In the high school work I put the emphasis upon the art side, upon utilitarian results, upon the things that seemed to me the minimum result in any kind of a high school. Some accomplish much more than was suggested. In the university, home economics seems to me to serve as the latest interpretation of that much discussed question, the education of women.

Recognizing her audience as college educated and interested in the intellectual progress of women, Isabel, in addressing the alumnae of Glendale College in 1911, made the specialties of women's education her subject. Her talk was published as an article in the *Wooster Quarterly* of April, 1911. In the fifty years since the founding of Vassar it had been proved that women could learn as well as men, and now the question was no longer one of brain power but of appropriate use of brain power. Since she felt that one answer to the problem of distinguishing women's education lay in her field, Isabel entitled her article, "College Women and Home Economics."

Out of two subjects, each so inclusive, it is difficult to select material for a brief address. Perhaps the time element is the one most easy to use in definite statements. It was in 1865 that Vassar college was founded, so we may say that the procession of college women has been marching for about fifty years and that in the past twenty its numbers have increased many fold. The past two decades have witnessed not only changes in the numbers of this procession, but also in its training, its ideals, its avocations and vocations, its recreations, its social activities, its religious practices.

As one has said of the college life of forty years ago, "We took four years of our youth and devoted them quite unconsciously to the intellectual life and to the ethical spirit. We sought and we gained, both from work and from play, each according to his desires and his capacity, an entrance to the intellectual life." Without "sources" in history or literature, without an elective system or research, without laboratories, seminars, or any of the paraphernalia of the modern college, "we acquired, most of us without being conscious of the fact, the rudiments of a liberal education." "We caught a glimpse of the liberating truths, of that wisdom which makes one not wholly alien or ill at ease in the silent society of the leaders of the thought and life of all ages, nor out of place in the company of those whose lives today are guided by the wisdom of the past and inspired by the vision of the future."

So much by way of explanation of the beginnings. Even the attempt to portray the past shows how alien its spirit is to that of the present day. For already I hear the ever-present question, "What results are there to show for these fifty years in woman's life and work?" In the midst of so much destructive criticism perhaps it is well to recount positive results of these forty years, so well summed up by President Eliot: First, that young women can carry difficult subjects as well as young men can. Second, that the physical vigor of young women is not harmed, but rather improved, by a college course. Third, that neither the morals nor the manners of a young woman are injured by higher education.

To these it seems to me there might be added a broader outlook on life, a keener perception of its relations, capacity for teamwork, to which numerous social and religious organizations bear witness.

We all know that along with these practical results has come an entire change of spirit and methods in the modern college. Buildings, endowment, laboratories, students, teachers, equipment of all kinds in a material way are but symbols of the inner change of form and spirit. One has represented the change in these words: "We have lost, the 'sweet serenity of books,' and we have not gained the freedom of pure research. We have lost the independence born of detachment from life and have not gained the poise of practical efficiency. We have suffered and are suffering from that distraction of spirit which always accompanies great and rapidly acquired gains, too large to be quickly mastered or readily put to full and easy use."

So much for the present situation, for the present unrest in the college world. It is well to have this history of forty years for a background, while considering plans for the present and future education of women. It is well to know that women have both brains and strength for the most difficult problems of higher education. Of course women have always known it, but to have proved it is another and quite different affair, one which ought to bear much fruit in school programs.

Years ago women's colleges felt it incumbent upon them to demonstrate this proposition, and so some energy was expended in developing courses of study as difficult as those given in men's colleges, while the women in coeducational institutions were very zealous in keeping step with the men so far as studies went. Gradually the truth dawned upon both men and women that this was not wholly a question of brain power, but of the use of this power, and that it might be desirable sometimes to use it in the same way and sometimes for very different ends. As Commissioner Brown has so well said, "The battle for woman's education as a simple human need has been fought and won. The integration of women's education has been accomplished, its differentiation has not been." And he regards the latter as a difficult task.

This question of the suitable differentiation of women's education has long been the occasion for a vast amount of discussion in print and in lectures, forums, symposiums, committee reports, and panels beyond number. Isabel Bevier's clear and straightforward approach to this subject was in sharp contrast to the foggy and unrealistic thinking present in many of these discussions.

. . . This then is the question still unsolved. How shall women's education be differentiated? When and where shall the differentiation begin? I do not hope to solve it, only to give some suggestions concerning its solution. As one looks at the splendid achievements of these graduates of thirty and forty years since in home, school, church, community life, one feels inclined to advise against radical changes, but as one talks with these women themselves of the devious ways by which "they have arrived" one finds them asking that other avenues of training be opened. All recognize that life demands from a woman today quite different activities from those of twenty-five years since.

Wisely or unwisely woman is more in the public eye than formerly, assumes more responsibility in civic life, in philanthropic organizations, has more economic independence, more social power; so there is an insistent call for training that will prepare for entrance into these various fields.

In coeducational institutions, with the elective system so large a factor, one finds an answer to the call in new courses in applied science, in economics, sociology, the family, social ideals, but for the most part the women's colleges have clung tenaciously to the traditional studies, modified to be sure, but yet not differentiated in any special way, but the industrial spirit bids fair to break all bonds and to make a place for itself in the most conservative institutions. One finds in technical and professional schools opportunities for secretarial training, and for social service workers. Indeed, this latter field seems to attract a very large proportion of present day college graduates.

One other new departure is making a large place for itself in the minds of students of life and in the school programs outside of women's colleges;*viz.*, that subject which forms the latter half of my topic, home economics. We have had forty years of college women and ten of organized home economics. Until the past few years, home economics has not found much favor as a college subject with the older generations of college women. Greek has been preferred to dietetics, *though the chooser was ignorant of both.* It has been exceedingly difficult for women trained in the old regime of family life and family industries to realize how much of their inheritance has gone out of the home life and training and how dire is the necessity that the child have an opportunity to secure this training somewhere.

It is a mere platitude to say that the industries have gone from the home; quite usual to rejoice that they have gone; yet that is only half the story. Where have they gone? Do machines or men or women or children carry on these industries? Under what conditions of labor? and, perhaps more pertinent still, what is done with the leisure so secured? Where do the individuals get the training they formerly acquired in these home industries? Family life may express itself differently in different ages and places but its cardinal principles — consideration for others, self-sacrifice, honesty and economy — are unchanged and must be learned somewhere. Where can you find a more suitable environment for comradeship and cooperation for worthy ends than within the family circle?

I realize that the term home economics is to some a "stone of stumbling," to others "a rock of offense" — that to some it means baking and millinery, to others old wives' tales. But there are people who (while not regarding it as a balm for all the woes of life), see in it a sane and safe program for meeting some of the demands of this industrial age.

Out of the ninety and nine definitions given for it, let us take a brief one, such as, *home economics stands for wise expenditure in the affairs of the home*. What does that statement imply? That depends on several things. Your definition of home: What is it? The place to go when the other places are shut? The place to sleep and eat? The place to dress in to go somewhere else? The place to have company? Is it not the center about which family life revolves, to which they come for rest, comradeship, and inspiration, the safeguard of the family and the state?

Reduced to simplest terms, its material basis is a *house*. This suggests architectural design and construction. For in the houses we build and furnish we give, perhaps quite unconsciously, our definition of home. Further, it implies a *knowledge* of the supplies of the home — food, textile fabrics, art, metals — because there can not be wise expenditure without knowledge. Henderson says, "If one does not know where one wishes to go, there is small chance of success in devising a process for getting there." Also it implies a knowledge of household processes and products. This means a fairly large knowledge of science, history, and literature.

Wise expenditure suggests a knowledge of the principles of economics. It is said that three-fourths of all money expended is expended by women or for women. Why, then, should they not learn *how* to spend? To be sure, much of this knowledge may be gained by one's self if one lives long enough and works at it assiduously, but is there any good reason why women's colleges, aided and abetted by their alumnae, should not give themselves seriously to the study of the kinds of education adapted to present day needs?

Let us quote further the words of Commissioner Brown: "There will be some day preparation for mother-work, for homemaking, for woman's leading part in the finer forms of social intercourse, which will do on the higher academic plane what was done in a more petty way generations ago in popular finishing schools for girls. There is to be further a serious preparation for woman's part in the economic, the industrial, and even the political world." Why not this preparation here and now?

Women are in the business of homemaking; they are in the economic and social world, yes, even in the political world. Have they had that training which fits them to bear their part well in all these places? Where have you had opportunity to learn homemaking? In high school? No. Because you were working hard at college entrance requirements. In college? No. You lived in residence halls with little even of home influence. In your own homes? No. Because you were busy in school, in church, in club; besides, you were not expected to do anything at home. The cook presided in the kitchen, in which sometimes, on promise of good behavior, you were allowed to make candy. Mother or the maid cared for the dining room. The laundry disappeared down the chute. Sewing was sent out of the house or to a remote corner. What chance have you had to learn by doing or even by seeing done? You may know how a well kept dining room ought to look, but do you know just how to clean glass, to polish silver, or even to dust well one chair?

Some of you who are in your own homes can recall, I am sure, the time when you realized that the business of housekeeping was something quite different from a chafing dish supper or fine embroidery.

Under the present order not all of this knowledge can be acquired in many homes; if it is ever learned, it must be in school. Many of the schools are willing, but hesitate because of the additional expense. Just here, it seems to me, it will be well to correct some misapprehensions as to this question of expense.

It seems to me well to begin by seeing what material in the way of equipment at hand can be put to new uses. Good courses in home sanitation can be given with almost no new material in all our women's colleges — the same may be said for a course in applied art where there is already work in art. The library doubtless affords much material for a course on "the family." Economics is probably in the curriculum already and can easily be supplemented by a course on family budgets. History and literature courses can be made to yield much data about the place of women in family and public life. Current magazines supply much material for a course on the house — its construction, plan, and furnishing.

By all these an atmosphere can be created in the college and an attitude of mind which makes students ready for work on the home as a whole. In time a kitchen will be needed, but it need not be so expensive; that is not the chief lesson it is to teach. Rather it is to be a pleasant, convenient workshop, where intelligent people shall prepare food with economy of time, energy, and money; where respect for skilled labor shall be learned; where some of the first principles of the business of housekeeping which so many women work at or wail at shall be learned, so that the girl of today who is the homemaker of tomorrow shall not be so unequal to her task.

When we can do a thing well, it loses for us much of its terror. Ignorance is responsible for much of the bondage of housekeepers. It is found that by giving about one-fourth of the time usually spent in a college course to work dealing with the activities of the home, the girl may acquire a working knowledge of these affairs and yet have time for history, literature, art, and science. Thus she will leave the college halls better equipped to take her place in the world's life and work, whether she serve in the family circle or in the larger community life.

Chapter VII

In the Land-Grant College

MUCH of the achievement in the field of home economics, much of the general progress of women in the academic world and in society should be attributed, Isabel Bevier felt, to the distinctive contributions of the land-grant college. She was always glad to address the Association of Land-Grant Colleges and Universities and what she had to say was invariably well received.

In 1906, after six years in a land-grant university, Isabel, in the "vernacular of Illinois," told the Association what she knew and what she had seen in home economics. Coeducation, she said, had revealed to women a field of applied science belonging quite as much to them as to men. Aware of the difficulty in obtaining funds for a new department, she explained how little was needed for home economics and how the course work could be arranged to take advantage of that already offered in other departments.

When we recall that this talk given in 1906 antedated the organization of the American Home Economics Association by two years, we are again impressed by her original and constructive contributions to the evolution and widespread growth of home economics in the field of education. While thinking primarily of higher education for women in the roles they usually fill, she was always mindful of the important part the man plays in family life and emphasized it again and again. But she was a realist and believed that in most homes it was the woman who set the standards and was the administrator of the household.

Her address, "Home Economics in a College Course," is likely to be useful and pertinent for a good many years.

It seems like carrying coals to Newcastle to have one who has had but a brief experience of six years of the work of home economics in a land-grant college speak to those who have been a part of the work for thirty years. However, such as I have, I give unto thee gladly, and if the story seems too personal or savors too much of the vernacular of Illinois, it is because, being neither a prophet nor the daughter of a prophet, it seems best to speak of that which we do know and testify of that which we have seen.

It is not necessary in this audience to spend time in discussing the name or content of my field. Whether it be called domestic science, domestic economy, home economics, or as one Englishman put it, domestic knowingness, you understand that, reduced to its simplest terms, home economics includes those courses which have to do with the activities of the home along the lines of applied art, applied science, and applied economics.

This statement shows the work is not limited by sex lines — the facts of economics, science, and art are the same for men and women — the applications may or may not be the same. The home decorator may be of either sex, but must know the principles of art. In these days a knowledge of dietetics is essential for the physician — man or woman. Yet so long as the world is constituted as at present, the administrative side of the home is likely to be largely in the hands of women. It is said that 90 percent of money expended is expended by women or for women. Therefore the subject as a whole is of peculiar interest to women.

For our present purpose it seems better to consider the subject under two main divisions: (1) Factors in the development of home economics. (2) Its possibilities.

It seems to me much of the misconception concerning home economics has been due to the fact that comparatively few people have regarded it in its educational aspect, or considered it in its relation to other subjects of the college curriculum. It has been to many, a stone over which they have stumbled, but have passed on without stopping to consider whence it came. Closer study reveals the fact that home economics as it now exists in our colleges and universities is a part of a general educational movement, that several factors have contributed to its development. I name as some of these factors: education of women, technical schools, coeducation, changed industrial and social conditions, and the land-grant colleges.

Let us recall briefly some of the steps in the education of women. You realize that inadequate as the training was which was afforded by the reading, writing, and grammar schools that it was provided for boys only. Girls might be taught, but they were not to be admitted to the schools. The Dames' Schools were the only organized agency outside the home for the education of girls and they are said to have afforded opportunities to learn needle work, dancing, and improvement in manners.

It is interesting to note the steps of progress in the education of girls as evidenced by their admission to the reading and writing schools for one hour per day, of their instruction in the summer in arithmetic, geography, and composition, by their brothers who were Yale students and the various devices by which they were presented with the crumbs of education.

While New England led in provision for the education of its girls, some attention was given to their instruction in other parts of the country. The Moravian school at Bethlehem, Pennsylvania, is among the earliest. However, it was not until the last decade of the century that they were granted even a part of the privileges of the grammar schools. Special vocational courses at the Michigan and Illinois Industrial Universities were opened to women, while cooking and sewing were introduced into the schools of the Eastern states. The idea of manual training received a great impetus in the Centennial Exposition of 1876 and led in the next decade to the founding of schools for manual training in most of the large cities, the first being established in St. Louis in 1879.

By the close of the 19th century it was evident to the student of educational affairs that the industrial spirit in education was a mighty factor; that courses in applied science and applied art (their interpretation and application to the activities of daily life) would have a place in the school programs and that a knowledge of the classics was no longer the measuring unit for educational standards.

Women Spared Experimentation

While much is to be said concerning the advantages of being the first to enter a new field there are compensations for being behindtime. The fact that the education of women has lagged behind that of the men has saved much experimenting on the women. The technical schools for men practically settled both the technical and educational value of such training for women.

It is perhaps difficult now to appreciate just how much coeducation and the technical schools have meant in the development of the education of women, particularly in work in home economics. To be sure, in the early days of coeducation the women were so interested in keeping step, intellectually, with the men that they gave themselves sometimes too strenuously to the joy of that privilege. Again, applied science for men as taught in the technical schools gave a certain definiteness to their work in science, which was much needed in woman's work in those lines.

A Color, Odor, Explosion

It is not perhaps too much to say that much of woman's early work in chemistry was a more-or-less indefinite playing with test tubes in which one of three results was expected — a beautiful color, a bad odor, or an explosion. She was not long in discovering that her brother took chemistry and bacteriology not because someone had told him that it ought to form a part of a liberal education, but because he expected to use this knowledge later in his work with soil or in the dairy.

Women were thus helped to see that there was a field of applied science for women as well as for men. They realized later that the laws of heat could be illustrated by the kitchen range quite as adequately as by the steam engine, that the life history of bacteria could be studied in many household processes, and that the chemistry of food was in many cases better suited to their needs than that of stones under the title, "determinative mineralogy." Thus there came into being the applied science side of home economics. Applied art was a later development.

For more than thirty years some of the land-grant colleges have had work in home economics. Iowa, Kansas, and Illinois were pioneers in this movement and from that early day to the present no one agency has been more effective than the land-grant college. In the past decade the number of such departments has greatly increased in the land-grant colleges until now they number thirty-six.

No one agency has seen the possibilities of the subject so clearly or laid for it such broad and deep foundations. These colleges are, and have ever been, schools for the people — schools for the home. It has been their particular province to determine and interpret the principles underlying the work and the life of the farm and the home. Agriculture and home economics have had much in common in their development. Both are among the newer subjects of the college curriculum, so they have had to bear the questioning that is bestowed upon any new idea, the indifference of those who feel that "the old way is the best way," and the scorn of the student of the classics for "bread and butter education."

Home Ec. Not All Hot Biscuits

The agriculturist has had no difficulty in recognizing the need of the scientific basis in his own field, and he appreciates perfectly the necessity for it in home economics. He never makes the mistake of interpreting home economics as baking and millinery. As a result of the investigation and teaching of these colleges, the old idea that anybody can farm and that anybody can "keep house" has well nigh disappeared; and with it the idea that farming means plowing only and that the activities of the home are fully represented by the making of hot biscuits. Changed ideals concerning essentials in education, and the marvelous development of the work of the agricultural colleges have served as an incentive to better work in home economics, and both agriculture and home economics have steadily made perceptible progress toward better educational standards.

It has been well for both agriculture and home economics that their origin and their materials have kept them closely in touch with the people and so keenly alive to their needs. The spirit which animated the founding of the land-grant colleges was the spirit of the development of the individual that he might yield better service to the nation so that the nation's interests might be advanced. So the final outcome of either line of work has always meant better homes, better citizens. One great factor in the development of both subjects has been the generous support afforded them and the consequent freedom to try experiments that required time and money that few private enterprises could command.

It is evident then that in the varying lines of work included in the term home economics there is room for a great variety of agencies and very diverse methods of procedure. It would also appear that there yet remains to the land-grant colleges and the state universities the task which was peculiarly theirs in the beginning, *viz.*, the strengthening and deepening of the scientific basis in the work in home economics. It is theirs to determine the principles which underlie processes with which the world has long been familiar and to elucidate and interpret the newer phenomena in their relations. It is their privilege to dignify labor by sending forth from their halls, not farmers, merely, and cooks, but educated men and women who, because of their knowledge and skill in the practices and principles of the arts of the home, shall be able to use them as a means of expression for their best endeavors in the service of others.

The possibilities of home economics are limited by: the resources of the institution, the skill and tact of those who plan and conduct the work, and the attitude of those in authority in the college.

Plus Values in Homemaking

When one mentions resources, the listener is apt to think of the endowment fund or the legislative appropriation only. Few realize how much of the materials of the work of other departments can be utilized by the department of home economics or how much illustrative material can be secured from manufacturers for the asking.

As departments are managed in land-grant colleges, that of home economics is not an expensive one to equip or maintain. House sanitation, for example, can be taught in any reputable college with practically no additional expense. The same is true of chemistry of food. Only the other day the dean of women in a small college regretted that the college was debarred from having such a department by the additional expense it entailed and I felt that she did not appreciate how much might be done with the resources already at hand if utilized, and here may I suggest what seems to me is a frequent mistake in beginning such a department, *viz.*, the feeling that nothing can be done until an expensive kitchen equipment is secured.

It seems to me that the average girl in the land-grant college knows more about the food supply in the home than she does concerning the wise use of color and form and fabric in it and that much is to be gained by using the house, its construction and sanitation as the basis for the study of home and family life. The food supply takes its place then as one of the factors in the home life and work. Her love of beauty, her sense of form and color, the necessity of a knowledge of fabrics and furniture, are all brought into use in the furnishing of this house. And all the while the student is helped to a better appreciation of the meaning of home and family.

With regard to skill, tact, and knowledge of those who direct the work, out of all that might be said on this subject I prefer to select only a few points which seem to me general principles. If the field includes applied art, economics, and science the need for specialists is quite evident. No one individual could be expected to have sufficient knowledge. The work of organization leaves little time for the research needed to meet the questions that come to such departments daily.

Dietetics and Decoration

Dietetics in these days does not mean fads and foibles about food. It means the latest and best information the chemist, physiologist, and cook can give us about the composition, preparation, and digestion of food. *Decoration* does not mean a little daubing of color on china, but rather a knowledge of the principles of architecture, art, and design, with ability to portray color and form. Henderson says, "If one does not know where one wishes to go there is small chance of success in devising a successful program for getting there." So if one is to apply science one must know pure science.

It is said that Boston is not so much a place as an attitude of mind. It is particularly true of home economics that it is an attitude of mind. Some college authorities seem to act on the supposition that a thousand dollar kitchen and a two thousand dollar woman will insure a satisfactory department. That is a serious mistake. Within the past month two such women have told me they felt that they were working against a stone wall because of the attitude of their co-laborers. The patronizing smile and the calm indifference are alike deadening to the work. Sympathy, appreciation, and helpful criticism are needed — not "passing by on the other side."

I speak thus strongly and freely because I have no grievances of my own. No one has had or can have more loyal and generous support than has been given to me in the University of Illinois. In conclusion, then, it seems to me you, as men in authority in land-grant colleges, can best serve the interests of home economics in your institutions by protecting and improving those courses.

At the semicentennial celebration of Ohio State University (October 14, 1920) Isabel gave an address entitled "The Land-Grant Colleges and the Education of Women," which was later published in leaflet form.

Fourteen years had passed since her address to land-grant administrators, just quoted. Her carefully prepared and convincing statements in the earlier talk had borne fruit. She had been called upon to give advice and counsel to some of these college administrators individually, as well as to the women administering the home economics programs. Few of the latter had the kind and quality of college training that Isabel Bevier had, and few had her breadth of experience and her qualifications of scholarship.

In the following talk she speaks with more assurance, having behind her twenty years of successful experience as head of the department at the University of Illinois. Her remarks are of particular interest to anyone wanting to know more about the development of home economics in land-grant colleges and its relation to the education of women.

The education of women is a subject of perennial interest particularly to men. It has long been the battleground of many conflicting opinions. In order to better appreciate the contribution of the land-grant colleges to the education of women, it may be well to review briefly some salient points in the education of women in the United States prior to the founding of the land-grant college.

Educational ideals in the early history of the United States consisted largely of those transplanted from the mother countries. This fact is clearly shown in the education of men, though it is not so evident in the education of women, because their formal education was about two hundred years behind that of the men. Vassar College was founded in 1865, Harvard in 1635.

Investigation shows that the present status of the education of women, however interpreted, is the outgrowth of many conflicting opinions. Deep down in their hearts many Americans have a good deal of regard for the German conception of women's education represented by their three K's: *Kirke, Kinder, Küchen.* In contrast, the following are the qualities to be cultivated, as given in 1793 by a Philadelphia divine in his *Letters to a Young Lady*: "A genteel person, a simple nature, sensibility, cheerfulness, delicacy, softness, affability, good manners, regular habits, skill in fancy-work, and a fund of hidden genteel learning." Again, there is the training which President Thwing said transformed the drudge to the doll, and in this connection it is well to recall the names of Anne Hutchinson, Abigail Adams, and Susan B. Anthony to show that something more than "fancy-work and a fund of genteel learning" was needed to satisfy some women even in those days.

Out of many notable contributions to the education of women made by women, three at least deserve honorable mention in this connection. Emma Willard had the vision to see and the courage to say: "The character of children will be formed by their mothers and it is through the mothers that the Government can control the character of its future citizens." So she sought State appropriation for her work.

Mary Lyon saw all life through religious lens and simplified life by one dominating purpose — the glory of God — but this meant also the best development of the individual and education was a mighty factor in this service. In order that the poor as well as the rich might have the benefit of education, she devised the scheme which we now dignify in our college life by the name of cooperative housekeeping, with the religious element, alas too often, omitted.

Catharine Beecher, with the prophetic insight associated with that family, supplemented by study and travel, saw the hopelessness of the situation for women unless housekeeping could be made respectable, unless it could be connected with the fundamental science for a basis and so interest the brain as a compensation for tiring the muscles. Her desires crystalized in 1852 in the organization of the American Woman's Educational Association "to aid in securing to American women a liberal education, honorable position, and remunerative employment," or, in the phraseology of today, economic independence for women.

From this review it would appear that several points about woman's education were settled by 1865. First, that something more than morals and manners and genteel learning must be offered them. Second, the coeducation was a safe experiment. (In this battle Ohio has an honorable record. Oberlin was the first college to open its doors to women.) Third, that the work at Mt. Holyoke had borne fruit and a real college for women (Vassar) was about to be opened. Fourth, the pioneer life had necessitated comradeship in work and made possible comradeship in education. It would appear that the time was ripe for a new instrument of education that should embody these ideals.

We come now to the work of the land-grant college in the education of women.

These colleges were born in the minds of men who had the vision to see life whole and large. The land-grant college was a protest against narrowness in education, as the statement, "while not excluding the classics, but adding agriculture and mechanic arts," shows. These leaders recognized that a democracy demands that all the people be educated and that a task so great could be met only by national resources. So, it seems to me, the first contribution which the land-grant college made to home economics was latitude in education; breadth.

A glance at the beginnings of our land-grant colleges shows that in the decade between 1865 and 1875 the greater part of them were founded and that almost immediately the doors of those in the West were opened to women. It is difficult to overestimate the importance of this *second* contribution to the education of women. It is a far cry from the time when Noah Webster in his *Letters to Young Ladies* exhorted them "to be content to be women, to be mild, social, and sentimental," to the statement made by the Secretary of Agriculture in his report of June 30, 1897, as follows:

"Among the educational movements which in recent years have engaged the attention of the public, none has been received with greater favor than the attempt to introduce into schools for girls and women some systematic teaching of the arts which are practiced in the home. Many of the colleges of agriculture and mechanic arts, together with scientific, technical, and industrial schools, now maintain a department of domestic science. Cooking and sewing are quite commonly taught in the public schools, and cooking schools for women have been organized in numerous places. While useful instruction in these lines is imparted, it is generally recognized that much remains to be done before the teaching of domestic science can assume its most effective form."

On this occasion it seems desirable to give some specific information about the beginning of home economics in the land-grant college.

Through correspondence with these colleges it appears that the pioneers in the work were Iowa, Kansas, and Illinois. Iowa and Kansas have maintained some form of work in home economics since 1869 and 1873, respectively. Illinois gave courses in home economics from 1874 to 1880, the present department being organized in 1900. The Ohio State University has maintained this work since 1896.

One recognizes that whether it be in the home, in the community, or in the nation, an idea requires for its propagation money and equipment. The *third* great contribution was a place and equipment. Sometimes, in the beginning, this meant a basement or an attic room, but the splendid buildings set apart for home economics here, in Wisconsin, in Oregon, are tangible evidence of the willingness of those in authority to share out of their abundance or their poverty for the maintenance and development of home economics ideas and ideals.

Another contribution to home economics by the land-grant colleges has been courses of instruction. In his report of 1909 the Secretary of Agriculture makes the statement that he is chairman of a committee on courses of education in land-grant colleges, and that his energies have been expended on planning a four-year course in home economics and a one-year course in animal husbandry. I call special attention to the sense of proportion indicated in this statement. There have been people who would have reversed the order.

In the early days the land-grant colleges gave not only elementary courses in home economics, but provided for its further development by making a place for it in the graduate schools of agriculture.

The demand for carrying the instruction of the agriculture college to the farm was soon followed by the request that it be taken also to the home and to the home-maker. It is a marvelous accomplishment of which most of us have no adequate conception, that the women throughout the length and breadth of the land may get, through their connection with the land-grant colleges, the latest scientific facts about the problems of their daily life. The extension service with all its faults has made a tremendous contribution to education.

Until 1914, although the land-grant colleges had made their contributions, had shared with home economics generously for the most part of their talents, their time, and their money, the federal government had not yet risen to the full measure of its obligation. The Smith-Lever Act is a memorable one for home economics because by it agriculture and home economics were written side by side in the records of the nation. Through this means the federal government proclaimed that it realized that the success of farm life was to be judged not only by the number of flocks and herds or bushels of corn and wheat, but also by the character of the home life on the farm.

And so another great door of opportunity was opened for human betterment; another chance was given for men and women, hand in hand, to work at the world's problems. That, to me, has always been one of the very great benefits that the land-grant college has given to our daily life — the fact that the men and women have worked together at the world's problems.

The recognition of the need of taking care of the women in the home was quickly followed by plans for the improvement of secondary education along similar lines. The Smith-Hughes Bill, to be sure, cannot be credited with having been written for the benefit of home economics, but when it came to put the ideas for which it stood into effect, the leaders found that home economics was recognized as so necessary a part of education for women that its claims could not be ignored. And so through our land-grant colleges we have another fund for bringing to the secondary schools the training of teachers in home economics.

The land-grant colleges have given not only equipment, courses of instruction, and training of teachers, but a large body of literature of inestimable value to the student of home economics. Scientific studies in the chemistry of food, physiology, specific investigation in meat, milk, wheat, wool, cotton, furnish a wealth of information to the student of home economics.

The work of the land-grant colleges was multiplied many fold by World War I. We were only fairly well started, speaking by and large, in the field of extension service when there came this sudden emergency which demanded that every man, woman, and child do his bit in meeting the terrible requirements of the hour. Again, the land-grant colleges, through their extension service in home economics, enabled the women of the country, along with the men, to stand in the first line of defense at home and by voluntary sacrifice to save food not only for the boys on the far-flung battle lines, but also for the women and children of other lands.

So much for home economics in the land-grant college in the last fifty years. What of the present hour? What shall the land-grant colleges do for home economics in this year of our Lord, nineteen hundred twenty? What Robertson says about sacrifice seems to me applicable to the land-grant colleges: "Do right and God's recompense to you will be the power of doing more right. Give and God's reward to you will be the spirit of giving more."

Four things, it seems to me, the land-grant colleges must do in the very near future for home economics. They will, I am sure, give more money, more investigations of wheat, meat, cotton, wool. They will work at the problems of food because the demand is so insistent, but I want them to work, and I believe they will work, more definitely than ever before on the problems of shelter, of art, and of research.

Our country life must be not only attractive in its material setting, but there yet remains much to be done in bringing to the dweller in the country an appreciation of the beauty of that environment. The child must be taught a love for country life and for country activities. The war has emphasized the part that recreation plays in a well-ordered life. Our land-grant colleges and home economics have much to do in the way of glorifying the daily task and showing the possible beauty of its setting. We may not paint great pictures nor see the painter's work on canvas, but let us at least learn to look for and to find in the beauty of earth and air and sky that which shall lift us above the pettiness and littleness of the daily round. Let us make life satisfying, comfortable, and inspiring. This is to be no superficial contribution, but one that can come only from careful, thorough research. The world has been too uneasy, has lived too much in crowds in the past four years for the cherishing of productive work which requires time for thought. All of us need more or less to sit alone with ourselves, to have time "to think but one good thought."

So I believe the land-grant colleges will meet with increased appropriations and more careful consideration the demands made upon it. And, greater yet, it will give what has always seemed to me its greatest contribution — the attitude of mind, the willingness to investigate and to experiment, to separate the false from the true, to evaluate life and to enrich it.

In the early days of my own work, I very soon learned to distinguish whether passing visitors, of whom there were many, belonged to the land-grant college or to the traditional classical school, by the response which they made to my statement: "We are working at the problems of the home from the scientific basis." The man from the land-grant college said: "Yes, the home opens up a very interesting field for the application of science." The man from the classical school looked at me a little questioningly and said: "Yes, yes — are we a little late for breakfast? Are the biscuits gone?" In other words, the former understood my language. He had worked at having people understand that the activities of the agricultural college were not explained solely on the basis of plowing. Having spent $10,000 for investigations in the breeding of corn, he could appreciate that it might be desirable to spend $1,000 in the study of the home.

It would appear that the land-grant college, in addition to the task to which it has responded so generously, namely, the strengthening and deepening of the scientific basis for the study of the home, must undertake to teach something more of the art and the beauty as developed in the social and economic aspects of our common life. The land-grant college must send forth men and women who shall be eager and able to use their knowledge of and skill in the practices and principles of the arts of the home as a means of expression for their best endeavors and so enrich country life not only in material ways, but also in the finer and less tangible things of the spirit.

Chapter VIII

Educating Adults

ISABEL BEVIER believed in adult education. She contributed to its progress through her work in the extension service of the University of Illinois, through her articles for popular magazines, and through her talks to community groups and women's clubs. To her, extension work seemed the most effective means. Of the Smith-Lever Act she said that it "unified, multiplied, and organized scattered efforts into one mighty force for adult education."

On November 12, 1919, she presented in Chicago at a meeting of the Association of Land-Grant Colleges and Universities, a paper on "The Illinois Scheme for Extension Work with Women." Aware that for many women World War I had meant excitement and activity and the feeling of participation in a great movement, she planned her extension program to fill in the post-war vacuum. Reading seemed to her a substitute for knitting but knowing that some women would want the social outlets that war work had provided, she suggested they concentrate their energies on civic improvement.

It seems better that I should call attention to the points of difference in the work in Illinois. There are a few points in which we attack the problem a little differently.

First, in regard to organization:

The men and women in Illinois have separate organizations. The County Home Bureaus are incorporated under the state laws; the treasurer is bonded. We feel that the advantages of this method are that women are put upon their own responsibility to do business and must, therefore, learn business methods, so that they do get considerable practice just in maintaining their organization. Women are rather loath to undertake business and yet it is very essential that they should, and this method gives them practice. It is something of an undertaking to get incorporated. The women who go through it know quite a little more than they did before about business and on the principle that "every little helps," we think this plan has many advantages.

This is just another way of saying that the conception of the work has been too narrow. Home improvement is a very large subject, not to be measured in terms of recipes or meetings attended, so a special effort is being made this year to have the housewife work at the problem as a whole. And we are helping them to that vision by organizing the work in our own office under general heads, namely: organization, food, health, household equipment, clothing, and school lunch. We had time in the summer to really study our problem together, and this plan is the result of that study.

Then we called in our county advisers and conferred with them regarding the plan. The county adviser is supposed to show in her own office the benefits of orderly organization of work. The fact that almost every adviser brought with her one of her board members helps her in getting this vision of the work as a whole into her county. The county adviser and her board decide the ways and times in which these different parts shall be studied, and when they are studied the relation of the part to the whole is carefully considered. For example, in the food work we are not giving a recipe, neither are we giving demonstrations as such. We are talking about food, first through Doctor Langworthy's chart of the great classes and functions; then we may have a lesson on milk, on vegetables, on meats. But in every case the class, the use, the cost and the relationships are shown.

144

So much for the machinery of the task. There remains yet the third point, namely, the purpose of it all, and that is perhaps summed up best in the words: the glorification of the daily task, the growth of the individual, and the general betterment of life.

All of us realize how restless and unsettled conditions are throughout the world. The housewife has not escaped this general atmosphere. She had had a good deal to do in the past two years with "drives" and crowds, Red Cross groups, conservation groups, and child welfare groups. She has had many calls to take her outside the home. Now the banners have ceased to wave, the "drives" have been given up, the Red Cross rooms are deserted. Yet there are three meals to be prepared, and there is housekeeping to be done, but without the stimulus of competition. Nobody is going to check the housewife's product. It is to be eaten perhaps without a word of appreciation, to be taken as a matter of course. A very large question is, shall she be able to keep this spirit of service, this inventive ingenuity. What is to be done with the time that she has been giving to war work? Some county advisers have put this question directly to their women. All of us have that question to answer, and upon the way we answer it depends very much the atmosphere of our home, the benefit to us and our community.

Two suggestions are at hand. Part of the women's time probably should be given to rest. A good many women's nerves have been badly worn, and the first need is to get them in better condition. The second is to substitute reading and thinking for war work. With the problems that are pressing now for solution (and they will be determined in some degree at least by votes), it is necessary that women should learn to use this right of suffrage wisely, and that cannot be done without study and thought.

The community idea of service is growing and needs to be encouraged. Women can really gain a good deal of knowledge about the way in which their use of suffrage can be made effective, or defeated by studying the politics of their local community. Many women are totally ignorant of what agencies are used to get, for example, a safe water supply, clean milk, and sanitary markets in their own neighborhood. The question of civic improvement has many angles. It is for the women to decide not to attempt everything at once but along which line their efforts can be made most effective. The old motto, "Here a little, there a little," is to be made, "Here a little and then more in the same spot."

In a letter written to Isabel while she was in California in 1922, Dean Davenport commented, "What has interested me more is the recent development at Washington to which you refer, by which I understand the Department is putting together in one office the administration of the county advisory work in agriculture, the home bureau work, and the boys' and girls' club work. I understand they are trying to induce all the states to effect a single organization, putting all three of these lines of work together. I have made faces at this proposition as being thoroughly outrageous, particularly in home economics. I should like to know what you think of it."

He was not long in finding out and in a hand-penned letter using some of her characteristic expressions. She said in part: "Seems to me that is just Yankee Smith's (in charge of the Washington office of Extension) lack of vision. The Washington men are evidently hard pushed to retrench and being old-fashioned gentlemen fall to on the women.

"I'm inclined to think in the immediate future Smith will win but I believe in the end he will lose. After all women are going to have and keep a place in the world's work and the quicker men and women agree to work at the job together the better it will be for the world. I believe the Illinois plan educated the women and teaches them by making them bear the responsibility for their deeds — good and bad.

"Another chapter of the same kind has been written by Judge Payne, new head of Red Cross. They need to retrench. Without consulting anybody he sent a note dispensing with the department of nutrition. The one new department which was proved so necessary.

"Fortunately Surgeon General Ireland said he would no more think of doing without a dietetian in the army hospitals than a nurse. But even after a two-hour conference the 'Judge' was of the same opinion still."

Partly because of her early life on a farm and her later relation to the college of agriculture in a land-grant college, but quite as much because of her broad human sympathy, Isabel had a great interest in farm people. She wanted rest and recreation for the whole family, and, for the farm wife, pretty clothes, an attractive home, and the right to spend a little more than the butter-and-egg money. In 1917 she spoke to an audience in Ohio on "Problems of the Farm Family."

I can but feel that those who have had no association with some spot of earth in their childhood days have missed much from life's memories. Many farm couples who have left the land that was consecrated by their best efforts that they had as it were bought with the price of their own toil, have found the new house in town, notwithstanding all its new modern conveniences, an empty shell, because it lacks all the associations that had enriched the farm home.

To be sure, one may find a very different kind of reference to the farm. It is sometimes used as a symbol of all that is crude and undesirable, a fair field for the would-be social uplifter.

Modern Farm Life — 1917

In the midst of these conflicting statements, it is perhaps well to stop and seek for an answer to a few questions: What do the new farming and the new housekeeping mean? What are the problems and opportunities of farm life in this year of our Lord 1917 in this state of Ohio?

The new farming does not mean that men must cease to plow or sow or reap. The new farming means that these processes are to be carried on more intelligently because the farmer knows more about the character of the soil, more about the needs of different crops, and can secure helpful machinery. The new farming means, too, that business principles are to be considered in the work of the farm. The plowing and sowing are to be mixed with brains as well as brawn — with the latest discoveries about plant breeding and animal feeding.

Electric Dishwashers and Irons

We hear much in these days of farm organization. Farming has passed the stage when its bookkeeping was kept in a discarded copybook and its valuable papers kept on the clock shelf or in the clock. The new housekeeping does not mean that dishes will not need to be washed by hand. No one, so far as I know, has invented a dishwasher for the family that compares in efficiency with the work of the daughter. Beds will still have to be made, even if the sheets are washed and ironed by electric power. At least 1,095 meals will have to be prepared and served unless the family are invited out a great deal.

New housekeeping and new farming does not mean a discarding of the old just because it is old. It means rather an interpretation of all that was best in the old order into the new forms. For example, we shall not use less water, but more water. "The old oaken bucket, the moss covered bucket" is replaced by the wind-pump and the piping which brings the water into the house and so there is *less moss*, fewer tired muscles, and more water.

Attitude of Mind

The new farm life means an attitude of mind that recognizes that land owners are trustees of a valuable inheritance which they should pass on unimpaired. It recognizes that people are more than land, more than machines — that the purpose of the farm home and the farm life is to produce healthy, happy, useful individuals who shall find their satisfaction, their means of expression, their place of contributing to the world's joy, bearing their share of the world's sorrow, doing their share of the world's work on the farm or in the farm home.

Now for the problems.

The problems of the farm family, as of any other family, are connected with food, shelter, clothing, work, rest, recreation, citizenship, and higher life. Here, too, as with other people, undue emphasis is often placed on the first three, while the other three are neglected.

The farm home usually has plenty of food. It may lack variety from meal to meal. The menu may always read "bread, meat, potatoes." One woman told me three things always appeared on her table — onions, catsup, and crackers! This combination goes with the statement of the woman, "Planning of meals — nonsense, I have bother enough to get them without planning them." Here again the new housekeeping teaches that ten minutes with brains, paper, and pencil will save hours if it yields a plan of work. The food may lack greatly on the vegetable side, it often does. Too much meat and too few vegetables is the common criticism.

The farmer's family shares the common problem of securing clothing — suitable and adequate clothing. The love of dainty, pretty dresses is not peculiar to the town dweller. Some farm mothers, just as town mothers, have denied themselves adequate suitable clothing that their children might have what other children have. Someone has said, "If clothes do not make the man, they make him look a deal better after he is made."

Women as Spenders

It is said that women do not know how to spend money, to sign a check. Neither would the man if he had never had a chance to do either. Women have been taught to *save,* not to *spend,* and they understand saving the quarter or the dollar. The one pocketbook that belongs to father is the source of more heartaches and little deceptions than any other single element of discord.

Much yet remains to be done in the way of convenience and comfort as regards the farm home. It provides shelter from the summer's heat and winter's cold, perhaps in from two to four rooms, but it is still true, as the school boy said, that he understood the meaning of the frigid and temperate zones by his home. Statistics show that a very large majority of homes are not at all equipped for comfortable and efficient living.

The next problem in the series named is rest, and I think this a more real problem on the farm than many people realize. The traditions are all against it, and so are the long summer days. One must get into the fields early before the sun makes it hot, and one must stay after sundown when it is "cool and nice," and so the opportunity for rest is taken away from both ends of the day, and the noon hour is shortened to half an hour, and the overstrained muscles and exhausted nerves make men and women on the farm during the rush of the harvest season irritable and touchy. Sundays and rainy days are precious boons just from the standpoint of giving an opportunity for rest.

The farm affords an opportunity for early rising, for a fourteen-hour day if one wishes it. There are farm homes where the women haven't time to comb their hair before breakfast because no matter how early it is ready, "a little earlier would have been better;" neither is there time before dinner which must come before eleven, and so the day goes in one great "gasp to catch up." It was of this kind of a home that the boy remarked it was always either time to get up at home or if one were up it was time to "hurry now and do the chores."

It has never been clear to me why the laborer in town could keep his family by working eight hours per day, while the country dweller needed fourteen. I can but feel that a six-to-six day would mean happier, healthier living, avoiding the strain of rush and the nagging of hurry.

Recreation on the Farm

The term "recreation" is not a familiar one in the vocabulary of the average farmer. It never occurs to him as one of the essentials of life. Rather, it suggests weakness, waste of time, something quite unnecessary, and so no provision is made for the natural God-given instinct of play, and the farm boys and girls, left to their own devices, find recreation in undesirable places and form bad associations.

The crowds that gather every Saturday night in the villages are a standing proof of the desire for comradeship and recreation. We need community centers which shall study the needs of that community, who shall bring together the forces for good and make them serve the needs of old and young alike.

If the purpose of living is kept clearly in mind, if suitable rest and recreation are planned for, much is already accomplished toward the higher life.

At an annual meeting of the American Country Life Association held in St. Louis in November, 1923, Isabel presented a paper on family life. Although the topic was not of her own choosing, she gave it a great deal of thought, and what she said was well received. In commenting on the role of parents in maintaining high ideals in family life she stated emphatically that the father's interest and affection as well as the mother's is important to the character building of children. As was often the case, her common sense and perceptiveness led her to conclusions later established through research in psychology and education. The subject assigned her was "Suggestions as to the Contributions and Problems of the Father and Mother Necessary for the Maintenance of High Ideals in Home and Family Life."

The Modern Farm Parent

This you all recognize is a difficult and delicate question to discuss because at every point the discussion touches questions regarded in all ages as private and personal. Even in these days of "the repeal of reticence" many a man and woman resents, as an invasion of private affairs, any question of home and family concern.

The *maintenance* of high ideals is quite a different matter from having an idea of high ideals. Heroes often seem very far from that role to their valets. Most of us can live at our best for a little while but far too few maintain a high level day in and day out.

I name as the first prerequisite to the maintenance of high ideals of family life by the father and mother, the attainment of high ideals in their individual lives. One cannot give to another that which he does not possess himself. As someone has well said, "It all works round to just this: you can't have quality, you can't have charm in your material environment unless you put them into it yourself."

As the second prerequisite I name a recognition of the magnitude of the undertaking. I would have the fathers and mothers understand that this is a war in which there is no discharge, no summer vacation or eight hour day.

The Mother's Part

I would also have it understood that it is a mutual responsibility. Many men are quite willing to hold their religion and church membership in their wives' names. Many fathers are quite willing to let mother attend to the daily and hourly character building of the family and too frequently heed the call of business when adjustments of rights among the children need attention. Comradeship in work, play, love, worship, property rights, and responsibilities of fathers and mothers is yet to be worked out before there can be any adequate conception of the mutual responsibility in family life.

Tradition and custom have long assigned to the mother the heavier responsibility for the upbringing of the family. Training for parenthood even now is usually interpreted in terms of the training for the woman rather than the man; for the mother, not the father. I am not pleading for the same *kind* of responsibility but that, in so far as possible, they shall share and share alike in the *sense* of *responsibility*.

So much by way of stating the situation. Let us turn to consider some contributions of the mother to family life. Helen Bosanquet assigns to the wife the function of manager and spender of the family income, and the care of home and children. Further, the mother is responsible for so ordering the household that every member of it may have a home life which is physically healthy and morally wholesome; a well-ordered household she regards as a woman's first duty toward the partner, her husband.

Lita Bane's statement is: To have every home . . .

Economically sound
Mechanically convenient
Physically healthful
Morally wholesome

Artistically satisfying
Mentally stimulating
Socially responsible
Spiritually inspiring
Founded upon mutual affection and respect.

Another writer calls attention to the fact that "the mother and child form the first social group within the loose association of the herd; the first group to develop by virtue of its conscious relationship, the sense of trust and the habit of service of the stronger to the weaker." This writer names six points as recognized essentials in child care: (1) protection; (2) provision of necessities for the young; (3) drilling in physical habits and personal behavior; (4) teaching the child to walk, talk, obey, and imitate; (5) interpreting group morals; (6) formal education in folklore, vocational skill, and social arrangements.

I have spoken thus at length about the woman's part in the material development of the family life because it seems to me a prime essential. The knowledge of the technique of household processes by the mother is a very large element of satisfaction, not only to her but to all of her family.

Because of my life-long interest in home economics, you may feel that I am likely to stop a long time at this point to discuss the value of home economics training, but that seems to me quite unnecessary. I think it is quite generally understood how valuable this training is for every woman. What I do want to say is that the girl should recognize early her relation to family life and make provision for it in every possible way.

It is time we begin to teach the child the beauty and normality of family life. He ought to breathe it in from his earliest days. Physical, mental, and moral health are not three distinct entities, but one in the ideal life. Family life must be spoken of as something to be prepared for, cherished, cultivated as a delicate and beautiful plant.

A 1923 View of Communism

We are not in Russia but I was interested in this statement about Russia given in a recent magazine, "Another questionnaire circulated among young people working in one of the large Moscow factories dealt with their attitude toward family life. Several of the replies indicated considerable confusion in the young persons' minds as to what a family really was. Some confessed that they did not know. No one spoke of a family as a circle dear to one's heart where one lives among kindred who understand and love him. Most of the replies indicated little tenderness for the mother. She is defined as 'an educator,' or a 'person having authority,' or 'a cook.' Fifty-four young persons gave the last of these definitions. If the answers showed little evidence of affection for the mother, they showed no indication whatever of this sentiment for the father. In every instance he was defined as 'the family manager,' 'the food provider,' 'the worker,' or by some kindred term. Communists interpret these answers as proof that children brought up under modern industrial conditions never learn what family life and family sentiment are. Critics of the present regime in Russia attribute the character of the replies to the fact that young workers spend most of their time, when not at the factory, at their clubs and in other Communist organizations, and not only see little home life, but grow up in an atmosphere unfavorable to its development."

Individualism is to be cherished and developed but not at the expense of family life; club life and community life are not to be indulged in to the detriment of family life.

So much for the present as to training the woman for her task — now for the man's part.

The Father's Part

These same authorities quoted before ascribe to the man responsibility to the community of which he is a member for proper maintenance, and the upbringing of the family which he has called into existence.

It is a far cry from the absolute power and authority for life and death of the patriarchal father to the modern ideal. His authority is still great in determining the basis of family life, the scale upon which the household is to be organized, the kind of education for the children, and the place in which the family is to reside. His pocketbook, his occupation, his personal habits are recognized factors. About these extraneous matters there is quite general agreement; but alas, too often the preparation stops here.

What boy is trained for family life? The successive steps of adolescence and coming of age might be made sacred and beautiful portals to a new life if fathers and mothers worked to that end. The boy might be taught what the use and abuse of these new powers meant and how far reaching were the results in either case. For the adult man it seems to me the adjustment to the new order is even more difficult than for the woman. He has not had her training in adjustment, in diplomacy. From very early days woman has had long schooling in learning how to secure what she wished from her lord, master, husband. Power through money, politics he understands but this attitude of mind that the woman has equal right to self-development is as far as the poles from his daily thinking.

To summarize, the maintenance of high ideals in family life by the father and mother requires: the embodiment of these ideals in the individuals themselves; an appreciation of the magnitude of the task; instruction of the children in the normality and beauty of family life, its sacrifices and rewards, as a proper goal for their best endeavors; an appreciation by both men and women of what is implied in economic, civic, and social equality as applied to present day family life and problems."

In a talk given in 1910 Miss Bevier urged that the women's clubs, with their interest in developing "attractive and capable women," work toward bringing the home and home economics closer together. She recognized that in the twentieth century problems resulting from the industrial revolution were facing women in the home as well as men in industry. Many of the small industries, once the work of women and children, had gone outside the home, yet the responsibility of management and a major share of the work remained for the homemaker. No girl, she contended, should be left in ignorance of the skills she would need as a wife merely because her labor as a child was no longer needed.

Written when she had had ten years of experience as head of the Home Economics Department at Illinois, "Home Economics and the Home" carried weight then and is almost as pertinent today.

However much our opinions may differ in regard to the processes of education of girls I feel assured that there are essential points of agreement concerning the final product desired. The world has always needed and still needs attractive women, capable women — women who are able to do and to bear their share in the world's work, to give their part to the world's joy, to relieve some part of the world's misery. The place where they shall do this work may vary from time to time, may be in the home or out of it, but the qualities that make for efficiency in one place are valuable in general in all places, the incompetent woman at home may possibly conceal her incompetency for a longer time than the woman out in the world, but in the end "unequal to her task" is the label written large over both.

Let us inquire then what are the agencies by which these desirable products are to be obtained. The home, the church, and the school have ever been and still are vital factors in the education of the young. Each supplements the work of the others; each in turn is blamed for failure to perform its part. Just now one finds in current literature more of blame than praise for all of them. It is not ours either to blame or praise; rather to see with clear vision possible combinations of effort that shall make for efficiency. Somewhere every girl should learn the lesson of independence of action, of responsibility for her deeds, some knowledge of the essentials of living, power over environment, self-control, and ability to work with others.

A Plea for Religious Faith

I am aware that the influence of the church is discounted in some homes, neglected in others, and scorned in others. It is not my mission to defend the church. She needs no defense, but as one associated with young people, in helping them to a philosophy of life I am frank to say it seems to me most desirable that they be taught that certain fundamental principles are part of every life, that respect for authority, for the rights of others, individual responsibility, the recognition of a power outside of and beyond oneself are some of the marks which distinguishes man from the lower animals; that the Ten Commandments still furnish a working basis for life. It seems to me infinitely better to have a God to fear than to have none at all. Great indeed is their loss if they know not the majesty and beauty of the Psalms and of Isaiah, nor the comfort and inspiration of the words of Christ for their hour of need.

1910 Home vs. Pioneer Home

Let us glance at the work of the home in education. In earlier days the home was the center of a number of industries; the child had the opportunity of seeing these processes, of participating in them, and so gained a knowledge of them as well as an appreciation of the labor, skill, and ingenuity needed in doing them. Spinning and weaving were familiar processes one day, and when these went from the home the business of housekeeping — washing, ironing, sewing, bed making, cooking, sweeping, and dusting — was still the work of the family in which each daughter had a share.

Now the clothes go to the laundry or are sent down the chute to the basement, and the daughter knows nothing about them until she sees them clean in her room again. The cook presides in the kitchen, and the daughter is sometimes permitted to make candy in it. All the sewing possible is put out of the house; the rest of it is done by the seamstress in a room in a remote corner of the house.

The daughter is busy in school, in club, in society, but not with the affairs of the home — her interests are largely outside of it. She is exposed to judgment and taste far beyond her skill to emulate. When the real responsibilities of life actually confront her, no wonder she stands appalled at the task. It may be that by sheer grit and a strong will in a well body she is able to do and to learn until she has conquered her task, but how many fail and how many are made physical and nervous wrecks? Meantime housekeeping appliances and help too ignorant to manage them increase.

Certainly the mother who has had this experience will say, "My daughter shall have her chance at home and at school to learn and to do those things which are so certainly to be a part of her life." That does not mean that history, literature, science, and art shall not be studied and enjoyed for their own sake, but that along with them shall be taken work in lines that shall serve to make household processes and products familiar.

An omelet lesson in the school kitchen may serve as an application of the laws of heat to food materials, while it gives real skill in manipulation, control over materials and savory food useful to the family. A simple gown, well designed, neatly put together, of good color, combines knowledge of materials, of form, color, of wise expenditure that is well worth while to the woman in her home.

I am not pleading for a trade school, a technical school, or a vocational school — these are special forms of education. I am talking about women and their business of housekeeping and homemaking and the part that girls ought to have in it. It seems to me very much yet remains to be done before we women can feel that we are making a very creditable showing and, I ask, is it not time that the woman in the home and the woman in the school combine to make better the living conditions for all people by both better homes and schools? Let us have cleaner streets, more parks and better ones, do away with the unsightly billboard, the ugly bridge, the smoke, and the noise. But let us also have better bread, less canned meat and bric-a-brac, more real art and beauty.

Opportunity Lies at Home

Let those who have leisure, executive ability, and means go outside the home and better the environment, but let many of us stay inside until we have made these places real homes, not places to sleep in, nor to dress in to go somewhere else, but the real center of the activity of the family — the place of noble inspirations, of rest, and of peace. Let the lessons at school be practised in the home. Do not make the high school girl feel that home and school are working for entirely different results.

Where shall this cooperation begin? In the elementary grades — for many a girl will leave before she reaches even the seventh grade. You know how much a ten-year-old daughter does in many a home. She is housekeeper, nurse, and general caretaker. It is possible for her to learn in the public school how to use a needle, how to cut and care for clothes, how to buy and prepare well-cooked food. It is possible for her to be taught to do some *intelligent* thinking about it, to get an attitude of mind concerning such work. And in that she is often far ahead of her older and richer sisters.

I wish the homes to do elementary work too. Some of them are suffering greatly from a wrong attitude of mind. This business of living belongs to rich and poor, high and low alike. The tools may differ, but the business remains, and the apprenticeship should be served in all homes. If we could have for ten years the right attitude of mind about housework in home and school, I can but feel that we would have fewer girls of fourteen eking out a bare existence in any kind of an office or store rather than working in a kitchen.

It seems to me we had better spend money on prevention than attempt to cure after the harm is done. Businessmen agree that neither the boy nor girl is worth much to them in office or shop at fourteen. They have neither physical endurance, skill of hand, nor business sense. Then let us keep them in school, care for their bodies, teach them skill of hand, develop their power of mind, and so equip them better for the battle. Let mothers and teachers together study the business of living in their respective localities.

I do not mean by this a mothers' association that shall meet and relieve their minds by saying all the adverse things they can about the schools, draft a constitution and by-laws, and begin a gentle nagging process. Many associations need to have secret meetings for six months and learn how to work with each other and plan some definite thing to do before they can have anything worth presenting to the public.

Let mothers and teachers study the problems of living and the means by which the elementary and high schools can help in the business. Do not let the college take four years of your daughter's life and send her back to you less able and far less willing to take her place in the family life than before.

Women's Colleges

I can but feel that some day the women's colleges will see that they lost a great opportunity to be leaders in the education of women when they ignored the fact that it was their privilege to go out into new fields of learning and find those that should enrich and ennoble the lives of women rather than blindly imitate the colleges for men. It is not a question of more brain power or of less brain power, but it is a question of a different life and therefore of a different preparation.

"The functions of men and women in society are different in many ways. Do those differences lie wholly beyond the range of education? I am confident that they cannot permanently be left outside of the range of education, but the task of bringing them under educational treatment is one of the greatest difficulty. It calls for the highest exercise of inventive skill and patience.

"In coeducational institutions, under a system of free election, the problem tends to solve itself by the gravitation of women toward certain courses and of men toward certain other courses, while still other courses are common ground. But this solution is only partial and unsatisfactory. Some practicable scheme of preparation for mother-work will, we cannot doubt, be devised in the course of time. There will be, some day, an education for homemaking and for woman's leading part in the finer forms of social intercourse, which will do on the higher academic plane what was done in a more petty way, generations ago, in popular finishing schools for girls.

"But this, too, is only a part. There is to be, further, a serious preparation for woman's part in the economic, the industrial, and even the political world. What the all-round solution of this problem will be I cannot tell nor even guess. But if it meets the need, it will be an educational invention of the highest order of excellence."*

Note on Sociology

It seems to me reasonable to believe that many of these young women college graduates full of zeal to enter schools of philanthropy, be dignified with the title of social workers, and have experiences in slums and dancehalls, would do much more effective service if they had served an apprenticeship as social workers within the circle of their own family, and so "tried out" some of their theories.

It must be clear to you that I still expect the home, the church,

---

*Dr. Elmer E. Brown, U.S. Commissioner of Ed., published in Science N.S., Vol. 26, p. 168, Aug. 9, 1907.

and the school to educate the girl, but I ask for closer cooperation: that they shall learn not only history, literature, science and art, but the place of woman in the family life, the essentials of food, clothing, and shelter, acquire skill of hand, business sense by the actual work in public school, home, and within the college walls; that they may be able to serve with the hands in ordinary household process, while they fail not in keenness of intellect or in the finer things of the spirit.

Several paragraphs from an article, "The Development of Home Economics" *Good Housekeeping* (October, 1910), are inserted here because they emphasize Isabel's conviction that through home economics women can be educated both to be aware of their power in modern society and to use it intelligently.

To the woman in her home, interested in her kind and in the betterment of the common life, the story of the development of home economics in the United States is full of inspiration and significance. Because the apparent machinery — conferences and publications — of home economics of the present day is more largely in the hands of teachers than homemakers, this woman in the home sometimes fails to realize how mighty a factor she has ever been, and still is, in the real progress of the subject. The unnumbered words that have been spoken, the countless articles that have been written in the past year about the cost of living, may not reduce that greatly, but they have shown, beyond the shadow of a doubt, the power of the woman as an economic factor in the home, and the imperative necessity that she be so educated as to understand her task.

Many factors have contributed to the development of what is now included in the term "home economics." In a general way, the facts of its development are to be sought in the life history of those men and women who have been able to discover the signs of the times in reference to home and family and have given of their knowledge and skill for the betterment of the life of their fellow-beings.

In the West the land-grant colleges have been the great agents in the extension of this knowledge of the home. Perhaps no other agency has seen so clearly the need of the scientific basis for the work or been so insistent in the demand for it. The present-day farmer realizes the importance of science in agriculture, so it is easy for him to understand that many of the problems of the home must have the aid of science in their solution. It is the growth of this sentiment that has made possible and sustained the department of home economics in state universities.

Technical schools for men increased the content of education, showed the value of special training, gave a certain definiteness to such training, and, indirectly, an impetus to the development of women. If the man could find special use for his physics, bacteriology, and chemistry, the woman realized that the same privilege was hers, and soon discovered that the kitchen stove was a more satisfactory and accessible instrument for her use in illustrating laws of heat than the steam engine; that while the bacteria of the soil were interesting, those of the kitchen cupboard were nearer and more important to her, and as for chemistry, soap, stains, food, dirt, an unnumbered host of illustrations could be taken from her daily life.

Coeducation gave to woman not only entrance to a large field of knowledge, but also a comradeship with her brother in this larger life and broader outlook which helped her to see more clearly where her peculiar field of effort lay. When once she had the freedom and the knowledge to choose her kingdom she preferred the home to the office, factory, or the platform; and a voluntary choice of subjects suited to her needs followed a better appreciation of her place in the world's life.

Sometimes impatient with what seemed to her the superficial activities of women's clubs, Isabel Bevier often expressed the thought that women might better begin at home to improve the health and happiness of the world. But that did not mean she had lost sight of women's civic opportunities and responsibilities. Far from it. She thought it was both possible and imperative for women homemakers to be constructively active in civic affairs. In a brief paper written in 1919, she gave her ideas of what citizenship should mean to women. The constitutional amendment giving women the right to vote had just been passed. Realizing that many women were still confused about their new role, Isabel looked squarely at the responsibilities and opportunities of "The Woman Citizen."

We are accustomed to the idea of woman as mother, wife, burden bearer, caretaker in the home, promoter of numerous activities outside the home, particularly in church and philanthropy. But the combination woman citizen is a new one and, it seems to me, a good one. Doubtless the term will suggest different ideas, varying all the way from the militant suffragette to the mildest of womankind.

To me it means that this woman who has been for many years an honorable citizen is to have the legal right to be called by that name. We all understand that women who have been interested in their homes and community have been in a very real sense women citizens.

To be sure, there are many who have not realized their opportunity and so missed the preparation and development which it offered. Those women are therefore not so well prepared for the obligations which the new order imposes. These women need to take heed of their ways. The right of suffrage for which some women have fought for years is not to be lightly esteemed nor carelessly used.

Citizenship means first and foremost an enlargement of vision to see at least beyond your own threshold. You are not assured of safe water and milk inside your own home unless somebody has guarded the source of supply. These good housekeeping practices are to be extended to your community, health of mind and body is to be promoted in the school as well as in the home, good morals and good manners are to be promoted in the community. Wholesome recreation, attention to health of the children, clean markets, clean railway stations, comfortable restrooms, are a few of the activities just over the threshold. A pooling of ideas, a carefully-thought-out plan of procedure, one step at a time, and considerable overtime work here await the woman citizen. So much for the small inner circle.

For state and national questions, a serious study of the issues is involved, and particularly of the relationships. The war showed that women could find much time for knitting or for any work with a real need behind it. I realize that it is much easier to knit than to *think*, but now the need is for some careful thinking. The soldier is not the only person who finds it difficult to settle down to the daily task now that bands and banners are no longer in evidence. But I am sure health for the individual and the community lies in the way of attention to the daily task.

Surely we as women cannot feel that we have progressed very far so long as the woman's page in our public press consists only of recipes, directions for making beads, or designs for clothes that make caricatures of the human figure. Go home and get your local paper to omit the woman's column or at least put in it one question of particular interest to the woman citizen."

In 1947 the university honored Isabel Bevier's memory by naming a building for her. In a ceremony on April 17, the Woman's Building became Bevier Hall, "Old Agriculture" became Davenport Hall, and "New Agriculture" became Mumford Hall for the two deans, Eugene Davenport and Herbert W. Mumford. Under the general title "Three Great Leaders as We Knew Them," a program consisting of three talks was given. A part of the tribute to Isabel Bevier is included here.

Isabel Bevier
J. Lita Bane

It was my good fortune to know Isabel Bevier first as a teacher, for I was one of her students, then as an administrator — as a member of her faculty, and later as a "retired professor," so called — and through the years a warm-hearted, generous, loyal, constructively critical professional and personal friend. As you know, she never really retired from any of these roles excepting in name, when she became Professor Emerita.

Well do I remember one of the last senate meetings she attended when she was about 80. She was in her place when I arrived. Characteristically, she commented that she thought our President, who was a specialist in ventilation, should see to it that the room where the senate was asked to meet was "aired out" before meeting time. "I even opened one of the windows myself," said she in the stage whisper to which she was addicted. Nor did she forget to speak to the President about this matter, and his good-natured reply reassured her. The well-being of the University continued to be her great concern, whether it involved proper ventilation or far-reaching educational policies.

[Review of career — omitted here.]

"Miss Bevier's" high courage, great tolerance, and keen insight were illumined by a quick and kindly humor. She was distinguished for the superiority of her intellect, the accuracy of her judgment, the fine flavor of her words, and the greatness of her generosity and kindliness.

In commenting upon the failure of one of her associates she said: "I believe it came about because she never had a great sorrow and she never had a great love. In her hour of trial she was found wanting." Isabel Bevier had a great love, a great sorrow, and in her hours of trial she was not found wanting. Her deep, abiding religious faith was always a source of strength.

Through the years, she had a continuing interest in her former students and affection for them. She kept in touch with them in all parts of the country and enjoyed their confidence to a remarkable degree. They could count on her understanding sympathy and her joy in their achievements. She had an unusual capacity for forming lifelong friendships. Quoting one of her Wooster classmates, "It was the genius of her professional life to train talented young women for similar positions in colleges and universities. To finish one's life with the assured gratitude and affection of a larger American womanhood, and with the consciousness of a multitude of uplifted homes is a consummation devoutly to be wished. For our friend, it was an achievement honorably acquired."

Finally, the charge she gave to young home economists in one of her later talks represents, I believe, what she would say to us on this occasion: "Revalue not only your material assets and liabilities, but the social and spiritual contacts also, and answer the call of this new day for women of courage and ideals who shall fashion for this new day the new home fitted to the needs of these changing times."

Chapter IX

"As We Knew Her"

"I CAN paint the *executive*, the *woman*, or the *scholar*. Which shall it be?" That was the question Louis Betts, the portrait artist, asked Isabel Bevier when in 1920 at the insistence of her friends at the University of Illinois she presented herself to have her portrait painted.

Her prompt reply was, "The woman!"

To those of us who knew her intimately this reply was the expected one. I have known few people who could give to that word "woman" the dignity, the warmth, the depth of meaning she gave to it.

Her choice led to the painting of a portrait that is one of the prized possessions of the University. A good likeness, it reflects the noted artist's skill and the appreciation he felt for Isabel Bevier. She chose a becoming dress of blue velvet and Betts added a white lace scarf. The whole composition is a very satisfying one. The portrait pleased Isabel, as it did most of her friends. This portrayal of the kindliness, the calmness that bespeaks faith, will be enjoyed by generations who never knew "Miss Bevier" in her exactitude as a teacher or in her vigor as an administrator, but who will always feel pleasure in this beautiful portrait of the Woman.

The presentation to the University, "in grateful recognition of the achievements of Professor Isabel Bevier during twenty-one years of distinguished service as pioneer and director in Home Economics," took place at a Home Economics celebration on May 21, 1921.

The portrait now hangs appropriately in Bevier Hall, which Isabel conceived and planned as the "Woman's Building," which she contributed so many ideas, and in whose halls she presided for so many years, not only as head of her department but often in a social capacity.

The universal appeal of the painting gave rise to one of the stories she liked to tell. Reproductions were made and some were framed and displayed in the window of a campus bookstore. The usual prints of Whistler's portrait of his mother appeared in the same window just before Mother's Day. When a student wanting a gift for his mother said he'd like one of the pictures in the window, the clerk naturally reached for the Whistler. "No," said the young man, "that other lady. I like her better."

Each of her friends finds in the portrait the qualities he most loved and admired. When Dr. Henry C. Sherman visited the campus in 1945 to give the first Isabel Bevier lecture, he stood quietly for some minutes before the portrait and then said, "She won that look of serenity and strength. Few people know as I know the difficulties she overcame in her lifetime." The portrait appears facing page 176.

Something of a *word* portrait may help to sharpen the focus, and with that in mind the comments of several of us who knew her have been included.

Lita Bane's Report

She was tall, a little stooped when it was my turn as a

student to know her. She was strongly built but not heavy. Her hair was white, her skin delicate, the kind that carries a pink flush even in the years past middle age. Her hands were expressive, gentle hands, revealing as hands often do the traits frequently disciplined out of facial expressions. She sometimes wore rings — not, as I learned later, because of their intrinsic value but because of their association with people or places that meant much to her. Her eyes were blue and she often wore shades of blue that set off her white hair, the color in her cheeks, and the blue of her eyes. She wore comfortable shoes and moved a little bent forward with a determined step that made us feel that she knew exactly where she was going, was on her way, and meant to be there on time.

Her course, "The House," in which I was enrolled was a revelation to me. As a high school student I had planned to major in mathematics in college. However, my friendly high school principal advised against it, saying, "It's not fair and I don't pretend that it's fair, but a woman in mathematics has to be ten times as good as a man to get anywhere. It's not yet a suitable field for a woman. Why not try this new subject, domestic science?" I had never before heard of the subject, and after two discouraging college years cooking tiny bits of food and making miniature garments for a model book, I was willing never to hear of it again. At this point I transferred to the University of Illinois and was fortunate enough to register in Isabel Bevier's course. Within a few weeks I found myself saying, "If this is household science, I'm certainly for it."

She reminded us that the house is not the home as the body is not the Spirit. Yet the house can be made to enhance and enrich home life just as the body can ennoble spiritual life. From there she led us to see some of the important phases of home life and what science and art can contribute to more satisfying, healthful, and inspiring family living. She thus gave us the educational philosophy underlying the household science curriculum as it was planned for us. And to me, the purposes of household science, far from seeming much too petty for college work, now seemed much too large to be encompassed in a four-year course. I have never since doubted the value of home economics as Isabel Bevier interpreted it.

In class, her humorous remarks were spontaneous and unexpected, and since she enjoyed them herself, they served to keep both her and her listeners in good humor.

Students found her intolerant only when they were unwilling to put forth their best efforts. When she felt the occasion called for severity, she could speak sharply, as she did to a student who tiptoed into class after the bell had rung. As the girl maneuvered toward her seat, Isabel interrupted her lecture to say, "You might as well walk naturally. We all know you are late."

Her severity was only for the moment. She did not cherish resentment and did not expect her students to. The heart of many a girl was warmed and encouraged in time of stress by an unsolicited letter of understanding and sound advice, signed, "Isabel Bevier."

She believed in her students. If she gave one of them a job, she had faith the girl would accomplish it. Consequently, her students seldom failed her if it was humanly possible for them to succeed. Often she inspired achievement far beyond anything they themselves dared expect. One of her girls, on being elected president of the Home Economics Club went to her and asked to be excused. "I can't face so much responsibility," she pled. Urging her to try, Isabel was on the front row at the first meeting of the club to give support and encouragement. This student, later a home economist of national importance, looks back to Isabel's faith in her as the beginning of her professional self-confidence.

No narrow course of study devoted largely to household skills satisfied Isabel Bevier's conception of household science, although she realized the value of skills. Day after day we found our horizons extending and our interest becoming more keen. To a student who suggested political science as an elective, her answer was "good," just as it was when another chose a course in Shakespeare taught by Stuart Pratt Sherman.

When in my senior year the time came for me to consider a position, one offered by a city Y.W.C.A. teaching home economics attracted me. Her comment was, "I suppose you think you're doing missionary work because you're with the Y.W. If taught the way it ought to be, home economics is missionary work no matter where it's taught." When after a year's experience I said to her that I had learned more in one year's teaching than in any two years in college, her calm rejoinder was that she always expected her students to. In college, she said, you were directed to reliable sources of information; but when you had to teach the material, you really learned it.

Soon feeling the need of more study, I came to Urbana to sit with Isabel on her front porch and discuss my problem. Study would be costly and my savings were limited. When I asked whether I was worth a master's degree, she answered, "You are one of my girls I hoped would marry and have a home of her own. Since apparently you're not going to, yes. I do think you're worth the investment. And

I know what you mean by your question. I've seen the ones whose money was wasted in advanced study."

World War I was upon us before my graduate study at the University of Chicago could be completed, and I was persuaded it was my patriotic duty to do "war work." My particular responsibility with the U. S. Department of Agriculture was to go from city to city urging the use of cottage cheese to save meat. When Isabel learned of this, she expressed her disapproval in no uncertain terms. There were plenty of people, she told me, who could work in the government's nutrition campaign. My own state had a greater need of help in its new extension program. Persuaded, I became a member of the extension staff when she was head of the Home Economics Department and vice-director of home economics extension.

She soon dropped the teacher-student relationship — we were now professional co-workers.

It did not take long to see what an influence she was exerting in the new extension development. Her sense of values, her own farm experience, and her faith in the competence of women were being reflected throughout the program. The work would be of better quality, she said, and more able leaders would be attracted to it if in the local organizations women were allowed to do their own managing and planning. In this she was whole-heartedly supported by the farsighted dean of the College of Agriculture, Eugene Davenport, and the equally farsighted vice-director of the Agricultural Extension Service, Walter Handschin; and the first county home bureau in the United States managed entirely by women came into being in Kankakee County in October, 1914.

In those days the choice of extension workers was made by a committee. On one occasion, after listening to objections to a certain candidate based on her not having lived on a farm, Isabel brought a quick decision by saying, "I'm not so much interested in whether the young woman has lived on a farm or in town as I am whether or not she has *lived*. I think this woman has."

Only projects requiring the use of a woman's mind, with or without the use of her hands, met Isabel's standards for an extension program. Proposals for programs devoted almost entirely to skills — and skills of little importance — were brushed aside despite urgings by some of the leaders in the national extension office and by some state offices. Isabel's favorite example of these trivial projects was one to make aprons from the tails of men's worn-out shirts. This, when there were so many worth-while things needing to be done.

My conception of the role of home economics grew as I worked with Isabel Bevier, and so did my appreciation of her as an administrator. Her great vitality enabled her to do many things and do them well; she directed her energies constructively and expected equally discriminating judgment from her faculty. One morning I went into her office just as another of her faculty was leaving, and she gave me a postscript to their conversation. Her comments on such occasions were half to herself and served as interludes between conferences. This time she said, "She sat up until two o'clock this morning, she told me, reading everything that has been said on the subject she's teaching her foods class today. I suppose she wanted sympathy, but I didn't give her any. A person with her training who has taught as long as she has should know who are the authorities on her subject and not feel she has to read all the others."

She valued the talents of her faculty beyond their use

in the classroom. It was her habit, and we found it a flattering one, to take advantage of them in her personal problems. She asked the clothing instructor to go shopping with her when she bought clothes, the home furnishing specialist to help with the choice of rugs, pictures and furniture, and the engineering research professor for help when her furnace misbehaved. She never questioned the propriety of her request, nor did her faculty. Many were the stories they had to tell of these "larks," as Isabel called them, for what to others might be merely commonplace to her had in it the spirit of adventure.

She relished celebrations of all kinds — birthdays, holidays, or parties given for some special event such as successfully passing a doctoral examination. For years after such festive events those who were there loved to talk of Isabel's pungent and picturesque conversations. Once she had the floor and knew her audience was sympathetic, her flood of comment and anecdote about staff members, wartime experiences with Herbert Hoover, and Trips to Europe grew increasingly delightful and often hilariously gay.

Occasionally faculty members who did not know her well felt her speech was too brusque or resented the dominant role she played in a conversation. She was given to diverting the conversation with great firmness and abruptness from channels she thought unworthy or that did not interest her to topics of her own choosing. Those unaccustomed to this habit sometimes needed a moment to land on their conversational feet, but the new subject was always an interesting one and lively talk continued.

Her associates sometimes found disconcerting Isabel's way of expecting one to know what she was talking about when she began in the middle of things. Conscious solely of the important points, she often hit only the high places in her conferences. Anyone associated with her had to be alert and something of a mind reader. She once called a faculty member to her office to ask, "What have you done with the paper that man left here last summer?" Not being able to recall having seen either the man or the paper, the teacher was nonplussed. Isabel looked at her keenly and said, "You stand there looking as if you never heard of the man. Don't tell me you haven't. I know you have." The bewildered faculty member walked out into the outer office and asked the secretary what it was Isabel wanted. The secretary produced the manuscript. When it was placed on her desk, Isabel said with satisfaction, "Now I knew you had it and would find it."

There was a personal magnetism and queenliness about Isabel that drew a coterie of personal and professional admirers. So marked and impressive were some of her characteristics of manner and speech that they were often unconsciously imitated. More than once a faculty member could be overheard saying to another who had spoken with unusual decisiveness or unexpected humor, "Now that's Miss Bevier."

Religion she felt should be put into use. During her residence in Urbana she was a loyal member of the Presbyterian Church. Her church life was a natural and unaffected part of her existence. One of her pastors referred to her as "a superb specimen of an intelligent Christian." She was not effusively emotional about her religion. She expressed it in generosity and thoughtfulness and believed it was needed to make life whole.

Many of her associates became her life-long friends. An experience that one of them had as a young member of her faculty is worth recording here, revealing as it does her courage, integrity, and faith during a time when her work was being attacked and her position at the University endangered.

Isabel had come to the University of Illinois with the understanding that she was to establish a department at the college level, one that would merit the respect of the entire university. She saw in home economics a discipline with cultural and professional values and she set about to build a department that would offer it as such to college women. In so doing she disregarded the insistent demands of the large and politically powerful group in the Farmers' Institute. This group had played an important part in establishing the department at the University, but saw it as a source of homemaking courses open to women regardless of their previous training. Institute leaders were not interested in a college department as such; they became critical of "impractical" courses in science, impatient with teacher training, and dissatisfied with the non-credit short courses offered.

During the first few years, criticism of the department and of its chief simmered. But in 1909 it boiled up and there was strong pressure to force Isabel to resign. Without doing anything to appease her critics she left on an overdue sabbatical leave. She had built as best she knew and asked only to be judged by her work.

A young faculty member, witness of her courage in this crisis, wrote:

"Unwittingly I was in the midst of the conflict. . . . I went to the University as a graduate student in the fall of 1908, found the work was what I wanted and worked hard to earn my degree. The next year Miss Bevier was to be on leave and she knew that opposition to her return would be at its height, led by the Farmers' Institute group. Yet, just as I was finishing my year's work with her she asked me to join the faculty for the next year and to represent her department in extension work, which at that time was done largely in connection with the Farmers' Institute. She did this in face of the fact, or, I like to think, because of it — that I was born in Illinois, as were my parents; that I had attended and taught in the State Fair School of Domestic Science under the auspices of the State Farmers' Institute; that I knew many of her severest critics personally and had been entertained in their homes; that I must know of their criticisms and would certainly, in my work with them, be subjected to subtle pressure to accept their view that she had failed to build the kind of department the people of Illinois wanted.

"I was young and inexperienced, but she did absolutely nothing to influence my opinion of the work of the department beyond that which I might have formed during my year as a student. Nor did she discuss the criticisms of her work, or ask my position in the controversy. The fact that I did support her position and was loyal to her department rather than to her personally (I had known her only a year) is unimportant here. It was wholly characteristic of the Miss Bevier I came to know that she asked only to be judged by the facts and had faith that right would prevail. But the trust she placed in me personally, making no effort to influence my judgment when she placed me in a position where I might have done her grave injustice, has left me with a loyalty and devotion to her that I have no words to express."

Fortunately for Illinois and for home economics, when Isabel returned home she found opposition fading, and in the end some of her critics became her strong supporters.

Isabel Bevier had a talent for warm friendship. As a

Wooster classmate and life-long friend once commented, "There was more in her life than the distinguished scholar and teacher — there was a woman of character, of force and tenderness, the loyal comrade and co-worker, the sincere friend."

Many people shared the friendship that Isabel gave so generously. Its quality and constancy are well illustrated by her never-failing interest in the family of a friend who had been her college roomate. The friend died leaving two young daughters, one of whom lived with Isabel during her four years at the University of Illinois. Isabel used to say that as she looked across the breakfast table she could forget the years separating them, for the young woman looked so much like her mother. Her friendship survived the friend's death by forty years. And it was a friendship that went beyond sentiment; she helped both daughters financially until they completed college and remembered them as generously on special occasions as if they had been her own.

Her friendships and her more casual encounters with people provided Isabel with her greatest recreation. With her home, her church, her books, concerts and plays, they so filled the hours not devoted to work that she needed no hobby. Unless, of course, one were to call her enthusiasm for travel a hobby. And even travel was for her closely associated with a love of people and of good conversation. The travel companions she chose were always interesting and her trips afforded her a fund of anecdotes to be shared later with her friends. Wide reading along many lines kept her informed about scientific progress, current events, and general literature. Her keen observations on what she read and saw gave her an endless variety of subjects for the conversations that gave her so much pleasure. As her hearing became impaired her face took on first a troubled and then an almost tragic look that told the observant that she was not hearing and what it meant to her to find herself out of a conversation, one of her chief sources of enjoyment.

But her fondness for travel, her interest in people, and her ever-present sense of humor carried her, in the course of her work, through experiences which would have proved trials for many women. She traveled about the state before the days of good roads and automobiles, when railroad connections were either poor or non-existent. The local freight, with a combination baggage and passenger car at the end, or possibly only a caboose, the long drive across country in bitter winter weather, perhaps with "three men in bearskin coats" as her companions, even the poor country hotel whose popovers were "raw holes burned on the outside," did not upset her. A hotel without modern conveniences was not a pleasant place to dress for a journey at four o'clock on a zero morning, and yet she managed to be a cheerful companion at breakfast.

Her great vitality, her good humor and, above all, her deep desire to improve rural homes helped her rise above creature comforts. Afterwards, in the warmth of her home her hardships became adventures, transformed by her keen wit and her gift for story-telling into amusing tales for her friends.

There were many other trips in addition to her extension work — trips to Chicago to shop for the department, and longer journeys for lectures or conferences that led to the four corners of the United States, to Canada, and even abroad. Yet the approach of vacation time usually found her consulting with friends or travel agents, studying maps, and planning a trip.

She once bought a lot at a Michigan summer resort, popular at that time with the University faculty, thinking she might like to settle down there for her vacations. In company with a friend who had bought an adjoining lot, she went once or twice to this resort. With the aid of a map and the guidance of a real-estate salesman, the two located their respective holdings in the woods upon a hillside overlooking the lake. They sat upon a fallen tree trunk while they critically eyed their trees and their soil. They admired the view and enjoyed the lake breezes, but neither of them ever built a cottage there. They agreed there were too many interesting places to investigate to tie themselves down to a single spot year after year.

Four times Isabel went to Europe, twice during vacation from college work and twice after retirement. On her first journey in the summer of 1897, just after leaving Pennsylvania State College for Women, she made the trip alone. But her sociable nature could not long endure solitude, and on the second day at sea she addressed a group of her fellow passengers in this way: "I come from a respectable family; I have neither murdered anyone nor stolen anything. I'd be pleased to enter into conversation with someone if there is anyone here so inclined." She was alone no more.

In 1907 she went again, this time with friends. Some conference, about which she later was purposely vague, gave her an excuse for the trip. The objective was not allowed to overshadow the recreational aspect of the journey. Her friends were amazed at her ability to combine shopping, serious sightseeing, and amusement in one day's program and yet appear at dinner full of energy, ready to give a gay account of her experiences. While in London, "to give her traveling companions a rest," she enlisted the services of another friend as guide for part of the time.

There were neighbors and church friends, trades people, students, and staff members who found pleasure in their frequent associations with Isabel Bevier. They saw her life, colored by her remarkable personality, in small intimate portions. They loved her but could not always estimate her greatness. There were others, for she had friends of many and varied interests just as she herself had such interests, who saw her life comprehensively against the background of her remarkable career.

Dr. Henry C. Sherman's Report

One of the friends who saw her life in its full setting was Dr. Henry C. Sherman. He was closely acquainted with her entire professional life, their friendship beginning in 1898, when he was a young assistant in Dr. W. O. Atwater's laboratory in Weslyan University at Middletown, Connecticut, and she was a student there. They remained not only professional friends, colleagues in the field of chemistry of foods and nutrition, but warm personal friends as well. When he expressed his affection by coming to Urbana to lecture in the Bevier series in 1945 he was Mitchil Professor of Chemistry at Columbia, a member of the National Research Council, and at work on one of his books, *Foods: Their Values and Management.*

Dr. Sherman once pointed out that as Louis Pasteur contributed through chemistry to medicine, so Isabel Bevier contributed through chemistry to home economics. Trained as a chemist and experienced as a teacher, she saw and seized the opportunity of extending the service of chemistry to the college education of women, first as household science and later under the broader term of home economics.

It was characteristic of Isabel Bevier, Dr. Sherman remarked, that she thought it best to organize this new department at the University of Illinois in close coordination with the established departments of science. Her students were taught the same foundation courses as other University students of science. No watered-down courses for Professor Bevier. Dr. Sherman also observed that no indication of any lingering desire to remain puristic appeared to bias the socially minded development of her new type of training. He added that she set the stamp of sterling quality upon the new coinage, and the scientific esteem in which home economics is held in any institution comparable to Illinois is closely proportional to the fidelity with which it has followed the standards set by Isabel Bevier.

Dr. Lafayette B. Mendel's Report

Another of her distinguished friends in the field of nutrition was Dr. Lafayette B. Mendel of the faculty of Yale University. When I first met Dr. Mendel he said, "You are one of Miss Bevier's girls, aren't you?" After speaking briefly of his admiration and affection for her, he said, "I'm going to use an adjective about her that I rarely use about anyone or anything — *sweet*. But I sincerely mean it about her. It seems exactly the right word." In his judgment Isabel belonged to that important group of American women trained in an atmosphere of science who ventured to give direction to the new home economics movement in a modern, constructive way. She was one of the pioneers who endeavored to translate current scientific research into the language of everyday life. This course called for courage in the face of traditional resistance to change, for vision and faith in what seemed unwarranted innovations, and for real leadership.

And so we have something of a word picture of Isabel

Bevier, the woman, the scholar, and the administrator. Like all portraits this one is not complete, but it will perhaps sketch the general outline in such a way as to give those who read these pages some idea of the deep satisfaction and pleasure that knowing and working with a great person gave to so many.

It is the portrait of a vital, intelligent, resourceful, dedicated pioneer in the home economics movement. Blessed with excellent health, an abundance of humor, great capacity for strong and lasting friendships, equipped with an unusually good education, she made noteworthy contributions to the rapid growth of a movement that was to become worldwide.

And Finally

Lᴏᴏᴋɪɴɢ back through the years of my association with Isabel Bevier, I find two of her favorite quotations recurring to me. One from the *Chambered Nautilus* of Holmes:

> Build thee more stately mansions,
> O my soul,
> As the swift seasons roll!
> Leave thy low-vaulted past!
> Let each new temple, nobler than the last,
> Shut thee from heaven with a dome more vast,
> Till thou at length are free,
> Leaving thine outgrown shell by life's unresting sea!

And one from an essay by Cornelia A. P. Comer:

> *"Here we have no continuing city. But when I am making my house live, I and no other, putting into it as I best may something of the serenity of Athens and the sacredness of Jerusalem and the beauty of Siena, then it is taking its place beside my greater loves. Then I am creating a home, not only in this world, but in the next. I have put something over into the eternal world that fire cannot burn, nor floods destroy, nor moth and rust corrupt. It is safe, even from myself, forever! No Heaven can be holy to me if I have not made this spot holy. I shall not ask, even from the mercy of the Merciful, a heavenly mansion if I have failed to make this earthly dwelling live. Eternity begins beside my hearth, shaped by my will. A woman knows!"*

Both of these reflect her own spirit and ideals.

"Gracious womanhood" was Isabel's constant goal, and many were the subjects of study she felt would speed young women toward that goal. She saw as an important part of her work the finding of courses that would be most effective in the shortest time, for four years is a brief period for study directed to so large a goal.

At this point, I find my mind going back to the day when, in 1912, as seniors at the University of Illinois, our class met with her for the last time and we heard her say: "But the final aim is gracious womanhood." The closing bell rang, "Miss Bevier" rose from her desk, and the lecture on "aims of household science" ended. The class in methods of teaching went its way. Some of us went far away, geographically, from the elm-shaded campus of the University of Illinois.

In the years intervening since that last class, the methods of making muffins that we were taught have been radically changed, the number of the then-known chemical elements has been added to considerably, vitamins have found their way into our vocabularies, styles in dress have changed and changed again, and "household science" has become home economics. But Isabel's goal of "gracious womanhood" still remains the final aim of all home economics teaching.

PUBLISHED WORKS

Following is a list of Isabel Bevier's major published writings. It reflects the areas in which she was most active and the points at which she placed her emphasis. Her early interest in research is noteworthy, as was her resourcefulness in preparing laboratory manuals and texts where none existed, her attacks on such pressing problems of homemakers as baking bread and roasting beef, and also her ability and willingness to translate research findings into practical suggestions.

Books

THE HOUSE, 1907. Revised in 1911. Published by the American School of Home Economics, Chicago. A compilation of lessons used in a correspondence course.

HOME ECONOMICS IN EDUCATION, 1924. Revised in 1928. J. B. Lippincott Company, Philadelphia.

HOME ECONOMICS MOVEMENT (with Susannah Usher), 1906. Whitcomb and Barrows, Boston.

Laboratory Manuals

SELECTION AND PREPARATION OF FOOD, 1907. Revised 1915. With Anna R. Van Meter. Whitcomb and Barrows, Boston.

FOOD AND NUTRITION (with Susannah Usher), 1906. Revised 1915. Whitcomb and Barrows, Boston.

Research Bulletins

Office of Experiment Stations, U. S. Department of Agriculture

NUTRITION INVESTIGATIONS AT LAKE ERIE COLLEGE, OHIO (with Elizabeth Sprague), 1900. Bul. 91.

DIETARY STUDY OF NEGROES IN EASTERN VIRGINIA IN 1897-98. Bulletin 71.

NUTRITION INVESTIGATIONS IN PITTSBURGH, PA., 1894-96. Bulletin 52.

University of Illinois

ROASTING OF BEEF (with Elizabeth Sprague), 1903. Circular 71 of the Agricultural Experiment Station.

SOME POINTS IN THE MAKING AND JUDGING OF BREAD, 1913. Bulletin 25.

PLANNING OF MEALS, 1914. Bulletin 30.

PRACTICAL SUGGESTIONS FOR FOOD CONSERVATION, 1918. Bulletin 22.

Magazine Articles

Journal of Home Economics

"Development of Home Economics." January, 1917.

"Experiments in Teaching Food Values." September, 1917.

"Reconstruction Days in Home Economics." August, 1922.

"Recollections and Impressions of the Beginnings of the Department of Home Economics at the University of Illinois." May, 1940.

Other Magazines

"Home Economics: Its Opportunities and Obligations." *School and Society.* May 20, 1916.

"Development of Home Economics." *Good Housekeeping.* October, 1910.

"Twenty-five Years of Homemaking." *Pictorial Review.* November, 1924.

Index

A

Adams, Abigail, 136
Addams, Jane, 93, 94
Agricultural College of Utah, 39
Allen, Lou C., 31, 32
American Association for the Advancement of Science, 79
American Association of University Women, 83
American Home Economic Association, 71, 77, 78, 120, 128
American Country Life Association, 151
American Men of Science, 79
American School of Home Economics, 78
American Woman's Educational Association, 137
Anthony, Susan B., 136

Appointment at University of Illinois, 24, 25
Association of Land-Grant Colleges and Universities, 78, 79, 128, 143
Atwater, W. O., 18-20, 22, 28, 34, 111, 180

B

Bailey, Liberty Hyde, 25
Bane, Lita, 152, 164, 167
Beatley, Bancroft, 100, 104, 105
Beatty, Miss, 47
Beecher, Catharine, 137
Bennefield, Eva, 60
Betts, Louis, 15, 166
Bevier, Andreas, 15
Bevier, Caleb, 15
Bevier Hall, University of Illinois, 164

Bevier house, 14, 15
Bevier, Louis, 14
Bibliography of Bevier's works, 185, 186
Birthplace, Bevier's, 13
Bosanquet, Helen, 152
Brinkerhoff, Cornelia, 15
Brinkerhoff, Henry Roeliff, 15
Brinkerhoff, Joris Dircksen, 15
Brooks, Fannie, 62, 63
Brown, Elmer E., 160
Bunch, Mamie, 59, 60, 63
Burrill, Dr., 30, 35, 36, 40

C

California teaching assignment, 81
Carnegie Foundation, 53
Carriel, Mrs., 44
Carter, Mrs., 43
Case School of Applied Sciences, 17
Centennial Exposition of 1876, 130, 131
Chicago Schools of Medicine, Dentistry, and Pharmacy, 33, 34
Chittenden, Professor, 52
Clark, T. A., 65
Colorado Agricultural College, 39
Columbia University, 53, 98, 99
Cornell University, 25, 27
Council of National Defense in Illinois, 62

D

Davenport, Eugene, 11, 13-15, 24, 29-37, 40, 43, 54, 55, 60, 63, 66, 67, 146, 164, 171

Davenport Hall, University of Illinois, 30, 164
Death of Bevier, 97
DeGarmo, Mary, 62-64
Department of Household Science, University of Illinois, 36
Dewey, Melvil, 71, 72
Dewey, Mrs. Melvil, 71
Draper, Andrew Sloan, 24, 25, 29-35, 46, 48, 50, 54, 97, 118
Dunlap, Henry, 48
Dunlap, Mrs. Henry, 43, 48

E

Eightieth birthday celebration, 95, 96
European trips, 83, 84, 89-91, 179

F

Farmers' Institute, 43, 44, 53, 59, 86, 175, 176
Farm life, 147-151
Federation of Women's Clubs, 46
Fitch, James Marston, 105
Fleming, Georgia E., 63, 64

G

Gibbs, Charlotte, 50
Glendale College, 121
Goldthwaite, Nellie E., 52
Gregory, J. M., 31, 32
Grindley, H. S., 36
Guthrie, Jr., A. B., 3

H

Handschin, Walter, 60, 171

Harvard Medical School, 16
Harvard University, 100, 136
Home Economics in Education,
81
Home Economics Movement, The,
81
Hope, Leona, 63, 64
House, The, 78
Household science
defined, 44, 45
origin of, 13
Huff, G., 65
Hunt, Ada, 62
Hunt, Caroline, 74
Huntington, Helen, 48
Hutchinson, Anne, 136

I

International Committee of
Women of the League of Na-
tions, 91
International Congress of Agricul-
ture, 84, 91
Iowa State College, 39, 79
Ireland, Surgeon General, 147

J

James, Edmund Janes, 49-51, 54,
55, 57, 66
Johnson, Lilian W., 49

K

Kansas State Agricultural College,
39
King, Mrs. S. Noble, 43
Kinley, David, 54, 55, 66, 88
Kluckhohn, Florence, 100-103
Lake Erie College, 23, 25, 28, 30,
38

L

Lake Placid Conference, 34, 36,
73
Land-grant colleges, 39, 42, 132-
142, 162
Langworthy, Dr., 19, 20, 144
League of Women Voters, 94
Leland Stanford University, 72
Lyon, Mary, 137

M

Magazine articles by Isabel
Bevier
"Development of Home Eco-
nomics, The", 161
"U. S. Government and the
Housewife, The", 113
Mann, Dean, 60
Marvin, Cloyd, 82
Massachusetts Institute of Tech-
nology, 21, 33, 34, 38
McCormick, Medill, 63
McDonald, Sir William, 40
Mechanics Charitable Association
of Boston, 113
Mendel, Lafayette, B., 52, 53,
181
Meredith, Virginia, C., 18, 19
Michigan State College, 39
Mineral Waters Committee, 19
Montana State College, 39
Moore, Ernest Carroll, 81
Morrill Act, 12
Morrow, Mary, 94
Mt. Holyoke College, 52, 137
Mumford Hall, University of
Illinois, 164
Mumford, Herbert, W., 85-88,
164

N

National Educational Association, 76, 79
Nelson, Mabel, 48
North Central Association of Colleges and Schools, 120

O

Oberlin College, 12, 137
Ohio State University, 22, 39, 78, 135, 138
Omicron Nu, 79
Opium Conference, 91
Oregon State College, 39

P

Packard, Bessie E., 63, 64
Palmer, A. W., 36
Payne, Judge, 146
Pennsylvania College for Women, 17, 19, 22
Phi Beta Kappa, 79
Philadelphia Museum, 43
Phi Upsilon Omicron, 5, 79
Plunkett, Sir Horace, 40
Professor emerita, 88
Purdue University, 78
Putnam, Professor, 18, 19, 21

R

Ravenhill, Alice M., 45
Raymond, Mrs., 43
Religion, 42, 156, 157, 174
Resignation, 66-70
Retirement, second, 88, 89
Richards, Ellen Swallow, 12, 21-23, 33, 34, 36, 38, 58, 72, 99, 111

Ricker, Dean, 36, 37
Roberts, Mary, 72
Rockefeller Institute of Medical Research, 52

S

Sedgwick, W. T., 21, 23, 33, 38
Sherman, Henry C., 98, 167, 180, 181
Sigma Delta Epsilon, 79
Sigma Xi, 79
Simmons College, 100
Simon, Cornelia, 46, 47
Smith, Albert W., 17, 20, 22, 23, 34
Smith College, 12
Smith-Hughes Act, 61, 140
Smith, Janice M., 100
Smith-Lever Act, 58, 61, 139, 143
Smith, Yankee, 146
South Dakota State College, 39
Sprague, Elizabeth, 23, 24, 38
Stanley, Louise, 84
Strain, Elmer, Bevier's fiance, 16
Swain, Frances L., 99, 100

T

Turner, Jonathan B., 44

U

University of Arizona, 82
University of California, 80
University of Chicago, 20, 74
University of Wisconsin, 74
United States Bureau of Home Economics, 84
United States Chemical Laboratory, 19

DATE DUE

DEMCO 38-297